PRAISE FOR

PEOPLE OF THE BIBLE: UNCENSORED

If you've ever struggled, failed, made mistakes or dealt with doubts, disappointments and discouragement, this book is for you. This book is about real people with real issues with real encouragement and real solutions. If you're tired of clichés and pat answers, the stories of the real-life men and women in this book will open up new windows of understanding. The practical "So What Can We Learn?" section at the end of each chapter will help you apply what you've learned in your everyday living. Christianity isn't wind sprints, it's cross-country, and Dave's insights will help you run a better race and finish well.

Gary J. Oliver, Ph.D.
Executive Director, The Center for Relationship Enrichment at John Brown University
Author, *Mad About Us* and *Raising Sons and Loving It!*

Here's a fresh look at the people of the Old Testament that will make them relevant to how you and I live our lives. My friend David Stoop has a way of making these people come alive. To see them as real people and not just characters in a story truly enhances studying the Bible. You will find new insights for daily living from these ancient personalities.

Gary Smalley
Author of *Guarding Your Child's Heart*

In this book, a seasoned Christian psychologist-pastor peeks at the darker side of the Bible's heroic Hebrews and finds the all-too-familiar matching threats facing today's people of God. The retold stories, penetrating and compelling, draw on the tales of the rabbis that imaginatively, and at times humorously, enhance the Old Testament accounts. Sound biblical interpretation, discerning pastoral insight, mature devotional counsel!

Russ Spittler
Professor of New Testament and Emeritus and Provost Emeritus
Fuller Theological Seminary

PEOPLE

OF THE

BIBLE

UNCENSORED

DR. DAVID STOOP

BESTSELLING AUTHOR & LICENSED CLINICAL PSYCHOLOGIST

Regal

From Gospel Light
Ventura, California, U.S.A.

Published by Regal
From Gospel Light
Ventura, California, U.S.A.
www.regalbooks.com
Printed in the U.S.A.

Library of Congress Cataloging-in-Publication Data
Stoop, David A.
People of the Bible : uncensored / David Stoop.
p. cm.
ISBN 978-0-8307-5727-5 (trade paper)
1. Men in the Bible. I. Title.
BS574.5.S76 2011
221.092'2—dc22
2011015184

Rights for publishing this book outside the U.S.A. or in non-English languages are
administered by Gospel Light Worldwide, an international not-for-profit ministry.
For additional information, please visit www.glww.org, email info@glww.org, or write
to Gospel Light Worldwide, 1957 Eastman Avenue, Ventura, CA 93003, U.S.A.

To order copies of this book and other Regal products in bulk quantities,
please contact us at 1-800-446-7735.

DEDICATED TO THE MEMORY OF WILLIAM GREIG, JR.,
THROUGH WHOSE ENCOURAGEMENT THIS BOOK
WAS FINALLY WRITTEN.

CONTENTS

INTRODUCTION

Stories are an important part of our lives. In fact, one could say that our lives are simply one long story. Jesus knew the power of stories, and most of His teaching was done through parables—a type of story. And the Gospels tell us the story of Jesus' life in the same way that the stories of the Old Testament tell us of God's relationship with His people, Israel. For centuries the stories of the patriarchs, along with the prophets and of several women, were told from generation to generation, to the point that these stories became a part of their lives. And the most intriguing stories in the Old Testament are the accounts of the lives of those patriarchs, the prophets and the judges.

My purpose in writing this book is to help you get to know some of the people of the Old Testament to a greater degree. I want you to see them as fully human; to see that they each fought to hold on to their faith in the midst of good and bad circumstances; and how, like each of us, they struggled to continue to believe God's promises. I think it helps to see that men like David wrestled with some of the very strong temptations men still deal with today. Some of these men suffered with depression; others with deep father wounds. There are even some who struggled with a sexual addiction, while others actually sabotaged their walk with God by their sense of self-sufficiency and pride. And, like us, there are some who became impatient with God's slowness to act, and who even doubted what God had clearly said to them. They each had ups and downs in their walk with God. Some failed to be the men God called them to be. Some of the men were heroes, while others were jealous of another's success, and some even sabotaged their relationships. And then there were the women—their stories shine like bright lights in the history of the Old Testament.

As a young boy growing up in the church, listening to the stories of the Old Testament characters, I became convinced that the people whose lives counted enough to make it into the Bible must have been perfect, even wearing haloes over their heads! I thought they must have had gigantic faith, trusting God for everything, and never doubted God. After all, God even spoke audibly to some of them. How awesome that must have been! I thought, *If only I could be a little bit more like them.* But then, I didn't read their stories very often, because I didn't want to feel guilty about my own imperfect faith.

It took a number of years for me to see these people as the Bible portrays them—good people who sometimes did bad things. In fact, some of them lied, cheated, stole and even murdered, and it seemed like they got away with it all. There went the haloes! But as I started to see them as imperfect people like me, I began to learn some important things from their stories. I discovered them as they really were—imperfect, flawed saints who cared about following God. Finally, I could identify with them.

Eugene Peterson makes this same point in his study on the book of Ephesians. He notes how often Paul calls all who follow Jesus "saints." Paul used the word in every letter he wrote, and it was an inclusive word. It didn't refer to a separate class of believers who were being honored by Paul. He said that we are all saints. "Paul deliberately chooses a word that identifies us by what God does in and for us, not what we do for God."[1] What Paul did with the word "saint" is what I want to do with that word. I want to look at these imperfect, flawed people of the Old Testament and, in their stories, find the nuggets of what God did in and for them, not just what they did for God.

What I have since found to be interesting is that the ancient Jewish rabbis who taught and wrote about these biblical saints never saw them as perfect. If anything, they did what I want to do in this book—they humanized them by fleshing out their stories, while at the same time never changing what God intended to teach us through their lives. For them, these Old Testament saints were very human, and in many ways very much the same as we are. Now, by referring to the rabbinic material in this book, I do not intend to suggest that these stories are inspired by God and have the same authority as Scripture. Nonetheless, the rabbinic stories do help us understand some of the full implications of the biblical descriptions of Old Testament saints. My intent is to make these Old Testament people come alive for you so that you can more easily identify with them, enter into their lives and learn practical lessons from their all-too-human walk with God.

Each of these people of the Bible whom we will consider had a rich personality. Most of them were men, as the Hebrews were a patriarchal culture. But there are women included as well, and they stole the show when they arrived on the scene. But whether it was a man or a woman, what's interesting is that they all started out with a lot of "holes" in their faith. Most grew to a point where they became "whole," and some even went on to actually be what we might call "holy." But their daily walk with God wasn't any easier than what we experience today. Each of these stories will touch your life in some way as you see how what they experienced is relevant to you and me today. So I challenge you to open your heart and find yourself in their stories.

1

The Imperfect Father of Our Faith

Abraham believed God, so God declared him righteous because of his faith.
GALATIANS 3:6

I started out in ministry as the head of a local parachurch youth ministry. Each week we put on a Saturday night rally, which featured as often as possible some well-known youth speaker with a dramatic testimony. I remember thinking as a young man how unfortunate I was to have had such a non-dramatic conversion experience. I often thought that I would have been a stronger and better Christian if I had undergone some major transformational experience. How much easier it would have been to have faith if I could see a strong contrast between what I was before I accepted Christ and what I became when I accepted him. At least that was the impression I developed as I talked with those whose pre-Christian life was characterized by major sinful behaviors from which they were miraculously delivered.

But as I followed the lives of these well-known speakers—they were all men at that time—many of them seemed to last a couple of years on the speaking tour, and then they disappeared. A few went on to develop ministries of their own, some of which continued for years. But I was surprised at the so-called "failure" rate. Over time, I saw that great faith was not related to a highly dramatic conversion, but was something we all had to develop over time. As an example, think about Abraham's conversion. Out of nowhere, Jehovah God spoke loudly and clearly to him. Now, that was high drama! If one could hear God speak that clearly, then surely one's faith must come easily. And for Abraham it didn't happen just once. God spoke directly to him over and over again.

When Abraham's name is mentioned most of us immediately think of the account of his willingness to sacrifice his son Isaac on an altar as an act of obedience to God. This was the high point in his faith-walk with God. Or we might think of his willingness to pack up everything and leave the security of his home to go to a place he'd never seen or even heard about, simply because this voice that claimed to be God told him to. Relocation was extremely unusual in the culture of that day—you always stayed close to home. Or maybe the most memorable part of Abraham's life was when God twice promised him an heir, and he believed God for that promise.

On one of those occasions, Abraham had an incredible experience—a visual confirmation of God's word. He watched a smoking pot and a flaming torch—a representation of God—pass through the pieces of the sacrificed animal in a covenantal commitment that God would do as He had promised; He would give Abraham an heir and land. In the days of Abraham, this ritual of passing between the pieces of the sacrificed animal represented the way a covenant between someone like a king and another lesser person was sealed. These three events in Abraham's life are highlighted in the New Testament, in Hebrews 11—that great chapter on the heroes of faith.

There is one other event in Abraham's life that stands out—the time he argued with God about Sodom and Gomorrah's coming destruction. What kind of relationship Abraham must have had with God that he felt he could argue on behalf of those two wicked cities! Where did he get the chutzpah to argue with the

Almighty, especially when in his argument he attempted to hold God to a higher standard of justice than God intended?

Abraham began his argument by asking God if He would destroy the innocent with the guilty. Then he asked God if He found 50 innocent people, would that be enough to spare the cities? When God agreed, Abraham lowered the number of innocent people to 45, then to 40, then 30 and 20, and finally down to 10 innocent people. Each time, God agreed with him. What courage to stand against God in that way! But to this day, this is characteristic of the way Jews believe they have the right to pray—they can argue with God. Jewish rabbis and scholars consider this right to be a part of their privilege because of the kind of covenantal relationship they have with God. We'll also see later that Job, the argumentative saint, was perfectly right, and perfectly comfortable, as he argued with God over his innocence.

I would guess that most of the sermons and Sunday School lessons I've heard over the years have focused on these four primary events in Abraham's life. But it wasn't until I started reading some of the old stories told by the rabbis centuries ago that I found there was much more to the story. Later we will look at what Paul said about Abraham, and what the writer to the Hebrews said. For now, let's look again at what Genesis says about this man Abraham.

What We Often Miss

We need to put the story of Abraham in context. The book of Genesis begins with two failures in mankind's ability to relate to God. First, Adam and Eve disobeyed God and were thrown out of the Garden. Then, one of their sons—Cain—killed his brother, Abel. Their sins set in motion patterns of sin and failure that led to God's decision to destroy everything and everyone with the Flood. The Flood marked the end of the first phase of mankind's relationship with God.

The second failure started with God choosing to begin anew with Noah and his family. But like the first failure, eventually mankind, because of sin, became enamored with themselves and started building a tower that was to be, as they said, "a monument to our greatness" known as the Tower of Babel (Gen. 11:4). Failure #1 led to failure #2. After God dealt with it and confused the languages of the people, he chose to start again—this third time with a man named Abram.

Abraham, at the beginning of the narrative of his life, is called Abram. (But for simplicity's sake, we'll refer to him as Abraham and to his wife, Sarai, as Sarah.) Abraham had a unique relationship with God. He believed that YAHWEH (the Hebrew word for God) was different from the gods that others worshipped. This God talked with him, and at the beginning of the account, in Genesis 12, God told him to leave everything and everyone and go to a land far away, a land that God would point out to him at the appropriate time. In that promise, God also promised that Abraham would become the father of a great nation, and that Abraham would be a blessing to others. In fact, God said, "All the families of the earth will be blessed through you" (Gen. 12:3).

We don't know what went through Abraham's mind. In those days, unless they were forced to wander because of drought or famine, people stayed with their extended family. But Abraham did as God asked him to do—he left his home with only the members of his household, his wife, Sarah, and his nephew Lot. The amazing thing was that Abraham was 75 years old when he started out. He wasn't just starting out in life, he was old at the beginning of the story!

When he finally arrived in Canaan, God told Abraham that this was the land He had promised He would give to Abraham's offspring. God didn't say anything about giving the land to Abraham, it was just a promise. And this promise is a theme that goes all through the rest of Abraham's life. For many years it is an unfulfilled promise. Abraham and Sarah were still childless in their old age, yet God was going to give them "offspring" who would inherit the Promised Land.

Now, if everything we have read about Abraham is true, his faith never wavered. But soon after he arrived in the land that was promised a severe famine hit. Abraham and Sarah have to head to Egypt to wait out the famine.

On their way to Egypt, Abraham, apparently for the first time, notices how truly beautiful Sarah is. The text says that Abraham said to Sarah, "You are a very beautiful woman" (Gen. 12:11) and Abraham became afraid. His faith was being tested, and he would fail the test. He was convinced that once the Egyptians, a people whom the rabbis said were a very sensual people, would kill him so they could have Sarah. So he made a deal with Sarah that when they were in a strange land she would say that she was his sister. Here's how the ancient rabbis enhanced the listeners' understanding of the meaning of Abraham's actions.

In his fearfulness, Abraham came up with a plan. He wanted to sneak Sarah into the country in a casket, and she agreed. As they came to the border, the tax collectors asked what was in the casket, and he said, "Barley." So they told him the tax and he willingly started to pay. His willingness made the Egyptian tax collectors suspicious, so they said, "No, you must have wheat in there. The tax is higher." And Abraham was willing to pay the higher tax on wheat, which only made the tax collectors even more suspicious. They kept questioning him about what was in the casket to the point that they accused him of having gold in the casket. And even then he agreed to pay the tax. They were so suspicious at this point, that there was nothing left for the tax collectors to do but open the casket.

One rabbi wrote that when the casket "was forced open, the whole of Egypt was resplendent with the beauty of Sarah. In comparison with her, all other beauties were like apes. She excelled Eve herself."[1] Wow! She must have been something else! The tax collectors were outbidding each other on who could marry her, but then they realized they had better report what was happening to Pharaoh. Pharaoh sent for Sarah, and he was so taken by her beauty that he gave all kinds of gifts as a reward to the tax collectors. And of course, Pharaoh gave all kinds of gifts to Abraham, making him a very wealthy man. At this point, Abraham panicked. He didn't plan on this outcome. And in his panic, he desperately and tearfully prayed to God for help.

But here's the point I missed for many years. Why did Abraham have to tell a half-truth, which was really a lie, to stay alive? If his faith was as strong as I'd always been told what did he have to fear? God had promised him offspring—an heir—and there wasn't any yet; so if Abraham was killed in Egypt, God was not God, and the promise was only empty words. In light of his faith, you would think that Abraham would be fearless.

But that's one thing that is so incredible about the way the Bible presents these Old Testament men: These men struggled with their faith just as we often do. Abraham was as human as we are, and when things got tough, his faith wavered and he depended on his own ingenuity rather than on God's promise. And this isn't the only time his faith wavered.

Let's continue the story. God sent a plague on Pharaoh and his household, which stopped Pharaoh from taking Sarah as his wife. Pharaoh was angry, and he confronted Abraham and asked, "Why didn't you tell me she was your wife?" (Gen. 12:18). And he sent Abraham away. The pagan Pharaoh confronted the giant of faith on his faithlessness!

When we come to Genesis 15, we see once again that God makes the promise to Abraham that he will have an heir. And to seal the promise, Abraham has that unique and incredible experience with the covenantal God. What he experienced was something that was very common at that time—a more powerful ruler would enter into a covenant with a lesser ruler by walking between the halved carcasses of a sacrificed animal. God literally did this with Abraham, promising him once again the Promised Land and an heir that would not only inherit the land, but an heir who would become a mighty nation that would bless the other nations.

Twice now, God had spoken to Abraham and made the promise to him of the land, an heir, and that he would be a blessing to the nations. The second time God sealed His promise through the covenant ritual. What we forget is that both Abraham and Sarah were even older now—too old to have children. Abraham was now 85 years old, and Sarah was 10 years younger—75—way beyond the age of menopause. Yet God had promised!

I think that perhaps some time later, Abraham and Sarah were sitting around on the patio to their tent, having a late night latte together, when Sarah notices the stars. She must have said something like this to Abraham: "I thought God promised that we would have more descendants than the number of the stars." Abraham replies, "God said it, and I believe it!" Then Sarah comments that in her devotions that morning she had been reading Hezekiah 3:1 where it says, "God helps those who help themselves." And then she adds that the other day, earlier in Hezekiah, she had read, "Pray as if it is up to God, and act as if it is up to you." (Both of those comments have a sort of "biblical" sound to them and may even be something you've heard a fellow believer say to you.)

Abraham asks, "What do you have in mind?"

"Well, I've been thinking. There's no way we're going to have an heir through me, so why not do what everyone else seems to be doing. We can help God out with this 'heir' thing by your sleeping with my slave Hagar. In fact, I'll release her to be a wife to you, and we'll fulfill God's promise that way."

The old Abraham took a look at Hagar and said, "Okay, if you say so." And so Abraham slept with Hagar and she became pregnant. Here is another test of his faith; and again, Abraham fails the test. As I read how Sarah reacts to Hagar, it has all the dynamics of Abraham's having an affair with Hagar. In fact, Sarah's attitude and behavior toward Hagar is so bad that Hagar actually runs away. It is only God who can get her to return to Abraham and Sarah.

Now, when the baby Ishmael is born, he is considered to be Sarah's baby, for in spite of her saying that Hagar could be considered Abraham's wife, Hagar was still apparently a slave. As a slave Hagar owned nothing, not even her child. So if you were a neighbor who came to see the new baby, you'd say, "Sarah, can I see *your* baby?" For 15 years, Ishmael was Sarah's son, and in both her mind and in Abraham's mind, Ishmael was the child of the promise. Together they had helped God out with His promise of an heir.

So 15 years later, when God approaches Abraham with a renewal of the covenant, and with the sign of circumcision as Abraham's part of this covenant, God in essence says, "You know, I didn't need your help. Ishmael is not the child of the promise. In fact, Sarah is going to have a baby—a son—and he will be the child of the promise." Abraham laughs to himself in disbelief and even defends Ishmael as the child of the promise.

To be fair to Abraham, he and Sarah had lived through many years of barrenness. The promise was first made when he was 75. Prior to the promise he and Sarah had struggled with being childless, thinking that as Abraham's wealth grew, his servants would inherit it all. Remember, faith is, according to Hebrews 11:1, "The confident assurance that what we hope for is going to happen. It is the evidence of things we cannot yet see." But for how long can we hope? How long can we believe something that is increasingly impossible? Faith is never a reasonable act on our part—it always goes beyond human reason. And because of that, faith is very fragile.

So it is only human that at some point Abraham and Sarah, in their impatience, want to see some evidence of what was hoped for. In the plan with Hagar it was clear that they no longer believed that the promised son "would be given." They would have to make it happen. We're not here to blame them, only to consider how human they were and how like us they were in the struggle to believe in spite of the obvious.

It is at this point that God not only renews the covenant promise of land and the fathering of many nations, but He also tells Abraham that Sarah will actually give birth to a son. Even as God says all of this, Abraham is concerned about where Ishmael fits in. After all, Ishmael is fully Abraham's son. God reassures Abraham that Ishmael will be blessed, but that Isaac, the son to come, will be the one who continues the covenant relationship with God.

Sometime later, the Lord again appeared to Abraham and renewed the promise of a son, Isaac. This time, Sarah overheard it, and she laughed as well. The big question for both of them at this point was, "Is anything too hard for the Lord?" A year later, they had their answer as they held the newborn Isaac. The impossible had happened.

But before Isaac was born there was another faithless lie expressed by both Abraham and Sarah, this time with King Abimelech. Abraham and Sarah moved to Gerar and lived there as foreigners (see Gen.

20:1). Abraham was again faithless and fearful, and he introduced Sarah as being his sister. It was the same situation as with Pharaoh. Abraham failed the faith test, even with the renewed promise of Isaac to be born within a year. Since Sarah was said by Abraham to be his sister, the king sent for Sarah and had her brought to the palace. The king did nothing wrong, but he suffered the consequence of Abraham's lie. A plague came upon his people. It was only when Abraham prayed for the king that the plague was lifted and the king could live. Once again Abraham was rewarded with additional wealth in gifts from the king. Soon after that strange, faithless situation created by Abraham's fears Sarah became pregnant, and Isaac was born.

What Sarah says about the birth is wonderful. Isaac's name means "son of laughter," and the reason is given by Sarah's words, "God has brought me laughter! All who hear about this will laugh with me. For who would have dreamed that I would ever have a baby? Yet I have given Abraham a son in his old age!" (Gen. 21:6-7).

Eventually, about the time Isaac was weaned, Hagar or Ishmael did something to Isaac that was offensive to Sarah. She demanded of Abraham that he send them both away. What a difficult choice, for from Abraham's perspective, Ishmael was as much his son as Isaac. But Abraham honored Sarah, and so Ishmael and Hagar were sent away. Again, God protected Hagar and Ishmael, but Abraham and Sarah now had their nice little family with no outside hassles.

Some years later—perhaps as many as 35 years later, Abraham faced the ultimate testing of his faith. It's interesting that the old rabbinical tales introduce this event in the same way as we meet Job in the Old Testament, though there is nothing in the Bible to suggest such a thing. They describe a conversation in heaven between God and Satan about Abraham and his love for Isaac, saying that Abraham loved Isaac more than he loved God. Satan dared God to test Abraham, and God did that. It was to be a massive test of Abraham's faith.

The Scriptures suggest that for three days Abraham and Isaac rode together in silence toward Mount Moriah. The two servants stayed behind a ways, and perhaps talked in hushed tones. Only Abraham knew what was going to happen. And for three days he was fighting within himself over what God had asked him to do. Questions raced through his mind like, *"Is this God of mine no different from all the other gods who demand human sacrifice?" "How can the promise be fulfilled if Isaac dies without even the chance to marry and carry on the promise?" "Have I been a fool to trust this God of mine?"*

But Abraham pushed on. Not only was his faith being tested, but his obedience as well. Could he—would he—do what God had asked him to do? All of heaven must have been silent those three days as they watched Abraham and Isaac approach the mountain, unload the wood and begin to carry it up the side of the mountain. Isaac finally asked the question that must have been rolling around in his mind for three days: "We have the wood and the fire, but where is the lamb for the sacrifice?" Abraham's answer must have torn him apart inside, but it was the answer of faith—"God will provide a lamb, my son."

Don't rush through the story, for it took time for them to build the altar and place the wood, all done most likely in silence. And then Abraham tied up his son and laid him on the altar. Then he lifted the knife and was ready to plunge it into his son's heart before setting fire to the wood. "At that moment, the angel of the Lord shouted to him from heaven, 'Abraham! Abraham!' Lay down the knife." And Abraham stopped! He untied Isaac, lifted him off the altar and then saw the ram caught in the bushes. God did provide the lamb to take the place of Isaac. What an incredible picture of how God would someday provide the Lamb—His only Son— "who would take away the sin of the world"!

The apostle Paul described the nature of Abraham's faith as his believing in a "God who brings the dead back to life" (Rom. 4:17). The writer of the book of Hebrews says that Abraham "assumed that if Isaac died, God was able to bring him back to life again" (Heb. 11:19). So, as the questions raced through Abraham's mind during those three days' journey to obey what God had asked him to do, he fought with the idea that God was able to keep His promise regardless of what happened on Mount Moriah.

There is also the question of how God could continue to be a righteous God and ask Abraham to murder his son. Perhaps

Abraham struggled with this question as well. A Jewish writer suggests that maybe Abraham was testing God.[2] Otherwise, we might wonder why Abraham didn't argue with God about this request just as he had challenged God's righteousness when it came to destroying innocent people in Sodom and Gomorrah.

Lippman Bodoff also suggests that perhaps Abraham was very deliberate with each part of the preparation for the journey, as well as the journey itself. He was obedient; but at each step of the way, he hesitated, giving God the opportunity to reconsider. It's as if Abraham said to himself, "I have found God . . . and my tradition and experience have revealed him and made him known to me as an all-powerful, all-knowing, just and compassionate God. But I need to be sure that this is the God to whom I truly wish to dedicate myself and my progeny and my followers for all time. If the God I have found demands the same kind of immorality that I saw in my father's pagan society, I must be mistaken. I must look further."[3]

We do know that Abraham didn't know the outcome until it was almost over. In his offering up of Isaac, we see the strength of Abraham's faith—the ultimate expression of his growing faith in God over all those years. He was willing to act in obedience to the very point of "killing Isaac—*with faith that I (God) would never allow that to happen.*"[4] Perhaps that is why he didn't argue with God on this. The test that God gave Abraham was also an opportunity for Abraham to test God to see if God was really God. And in this great test of faith for Abraham He did not fail.

Did Sarah know what God had asked Abraham to do? We don't know. But it does seem clear that when Abraham returned to Beersheba, Sarah was at Hebron, and she died soon after that. Then there was only one thing left in the history of Abraham—he had to find a wife for Isaac, to keep the promise alive.

So What Can We Learn?

One of the primary lessons we can learn from Abraham as we look at our own lives is that we are faced with the same issue that Abraham struggled with. Walter Brueggemann calls it "the crisis of deciding to live either for the promise" even in the midst of the barren places in our lives, or living "against the promise, holding on to the present ordering of life."[5] Do we live life with God's perspective, or do we rely simply on what we can see and touch—this material world. Brueggemann goes on to show that this "crisis" was a part of the ministry of Jesus. Luke tells us that as Jesus taught in the temple daily, "the leading priests, the teachers of religious law, and the other leaders of the people began planning how to kill him"—they were choosing to live against the promise, while "the people hung on every word he said" (Luke 19:47-48). They were choosing to live for the promise!

Abraham's life also shows us that the journey of faith is a serious one. It requires holding on to things we cannot yet see. It involves believing the promises of God in spite of the barrenness of the circumstances. Our faith is never perfect, but it should always be growing. All through Abraham's life his faith was dynamic, it was moving, growing stronger. Sometimes it seemed to lessen, even disappearing for a time, but then God would confront him and he got back on track. Ultimately, Abraham's faith, as well as our faith, will come up against the testing of that faith. Genesis 22 uses the words "God *tested* Abraham's faith." And for him, it was a terrible test—take what is most valuable to you, your son whom you love, and give him up! God may test us in some way, but what we also learn from Abraham is that when God tests, He also provides.

Faith is a difficult path to walk. Living for the promise is a lot harder than living against the promise. It's easier to live with what we can see, taste, touch and hear than to live for the promise of what can't be seen, tasted, touched or heard. For Abraham, it meant believing the promise of an heir despite Sarah's barrenness. For us, think of it this way. What is the foundation for how we live? Do we live like everyone else, holding on to what we can see, taste and feel? Is our way of life no different from that of our secular friends? If so, then we are living against the promise—our faith is not much of a factor in how we live. On the other hand, when we live as if we are pilgrims here, citizens of a world to come, and we are trusting God in the midst of any circumstance, we are living *for* the promise.

We, like the Abraham we first encounter, all too often vacillate between these two perspectives. At times Abraham lived for the promise. At other times he lived as a secular man against the promise. But gradually, over the years, his relationship with God grew, and he became more and more consistent in living for the promise. The secular lifestyle of Abraham receded as his faith grew. Eventually, his faith matured to the point where he could meet the test of faith that God presented to him. Eugene Peterson says the testing of our faith "is the catalyst in which our response to God, the raw material of faith, is formed into a *life* of faith."[6]

Obviously, God doesn't expect perfect faith. He longs to see us, like Abraham, grow in our faith. It will always include times when we struggle with our faith, and times when we live as if we are faithless. Unlike what I heard for so many years, it isn't that we just have great faith; it's that we choose the faith that will believe the promise. Jesus talked about mustard seed-sized faith. He said, "The Kingdom of Heaven is like a mustard seed planted in a field. It is the smallest of all seeds, but it becomes the largest of garden plants and grows into a tree where birds can come and find shelter in its branches" (Matt. 13:31-32).

Abraham's faith was like that mustard seed—tiny, uncertain, impatient, visible at times, invisible at other times. But by the time he was tested in regard to offering Isaac as a sacrifice, his faith had grown into a huge tree, so that in the end, God could say to him, "now I know that you truly fear God" (Gen. 22:12). His faith had moved from holey to wholly, and then, ultimately, to holy.

One more lesson from Abraham: In all of this, Abraham obeyed God. His test in regard to the offering of Isaac involved not only his faith but also his obedience. Throughout his life, he loved God; and as they walked together, Abraham walked in obedience. Jesus said, "If you love me, obey my commandments" (John 14:15). The walk of faith is a walk of obedience. What makes Abraham a saint is his obedience. He remembered that the goal was to finish well—to persevere to the end—and that he did.

The Silent Saint

It was by faith that Isaac blessed his two sons, Jacob and Esau.
He had confidence in what God was going to do in the future.

HEBREWS 11:20

I don't believe I've ever heard a sermon preached on Isaac. He could be called the "overlooked saint." He was certainly important in Abraham's mind as he represented the continuation of the fulfillment of the promise. That's why Abraham was so concerned that he find a wife for Isaac to marry, and that whoever he married wasn't to be a Canaanite woman. There is more in Genesis about the journey of Abraham's servant as he searched for Isaac's wife-to-be than there is about Isaac himself. But there is still much we can learn from what is depicted about Isaac, the silent saint.

I'm often amazed as I listen to people's stories about their families. My amazement is at the repeated patterns in the generations, and how unaware we often are about those patterns. A 35-year-old woman told me she had just discovered that her father had been living with a huge secret—he had been married before marrying her mom. But that's not all; he had a child in that marriage. This woman had just found out that she had a half-brother. But there was more. As she learned about her father from talking with an aged aunt, she also learned that her father's father—her grandfather—had done the same thing! For years in the grandfather's generation no one knew about his earlier secret marriage, nor did they know about the child from that marriage. Generational patterns repeat themselves over three or four generations.

One of the things we see in Isaac is the repetition of several generational patterns. Twice, his father Abraham had lied about Sarah being his sister and not his wife, and each time Abraham was rebuked, first by Pharaoh and then by the pagan Philistine, King Abimelech. I wonder if Isaac overheard his parents laughing about the folly of what they did in each of those situations. But then, generational patterns are often much more subtle than that. Isaac didn't need to hear anything from his parents in order to repeat his father's sin. It often seems as if the generational patterns actually end up in the DNA for several generations.

Isaac repeated the lie about his wife being his sister. There was a famine in the land, and Isaac was warned by God not to go to Egypt to get food, so he went south to Gerar, a land ruled by the Philistines. Apparently, the same King Abimelech, to whom Abraham had lied, ruled it.

While there, Isaac became afraid that his life was in danger because of the way men were looking at Rebekah, who, like Sarah, was quite beautiful. So they agreed that Rebekah would be referred to as Isaac's sister, just as Abraham and Sarah had done. The rabbis tell us that the old king wasn't going to be fooled again, so he kept an eye on Isaac and Rebekah. And sure enough, one afternoon he saw Isaac and Rebekah in the courtyard, acting like husband and wife. So he confronted Isaac, and Isaac had to admit he had lied. The King showed mercy and demonstrated more integrity than Isaac, and he guaranteed Isaac's protection—no one was to harm him. While living in Gerar Isaac planted crops, and despite his deception of the king, God rewarded him with a huge harvest, making him very wealthy.

Isaac differed from the other main characters in the family in that there is no record of God's speaking to him in a dream or in a vision. Neither is there any place where it says that God spoke directly to him, as He did with Isaac's father Abraham, and with his own son Jacob. Of all the patriarchs, Isaac is the least gifted in spiritual things. But it would appear that he worshipped God and was reverently faithful to him. He would be like the father who regularly worships and takes his family to worship but never speaks to his children about the meaning of his relationship with God.

Another thing that is only implied in the Scripture but is expanded on by the rabbis is Isaac's relationship with his mother. He was a mama's boy. He and Sarah, his mother, were too close. That's easy to understand. Sarah was probably a "smothering" mother, anxiously caring for her special son born in her old age—the miracle son. Naturally, when Sarah died, Isaac grieved. But the problem was, he didn't stop grieving. Jewish tradition states that you grieve for a loved one for a year, and if you grieve longer than that you are questioning the sovereignty of God. Perhaps that tradition was started because Isaac grieved for more than three years—so long that Abraham not only worried that he might not find a wife and continue the promise, but he was also worried about Isaac's health and even his staying alive.

The passage that suggests this is Genesis 24:67. As Abraham's servant was bringing Rebekah home, she saw a man in the distance and asked who it was. The servant said that it was Isaac, her husband-to-be. She quickly got off the camel, covered her face with her veil and ran to meet him. It's really a beautiful picture of love at this point. And then we read that "Isaac brought her into the tent of his mother Sarah, and he married Rebekah. So she became his wife, and he loved her; and Isaac was comforted after his mother's death" (*NIV*). Rebekah must have been quite a woman not to have been intimidated by the memory of Isaac's mother.

What We Often Overlook

At the heart of Isaac's character we will eventually find a man who is a silent father and, subsequently, a silent saint. His silence in all likelihood comes from the father wound he experienced in what was

Abraham's greatest act of faith. It was Søren Kierkegaard who first brought this to my attention. In his book *Fear and Trembling*, he wrote about this event from the perspective of Isaac, and I saw a whole new part of the story of Abraham's willingness to sacrifice Isaac.[1] In all the sermons I had heard about Abraham's great demonstration of obedience and faith, I had never heard anything about Isaac's experience of what to him must have been a great trauma.

What might have been going through Isaac's mind on the way to Mount Moriah? He certainly must have wondered about the sacrifice—where was the animal? *"We have everything we need, but we don't have a sacrifice,"* he wondered. *"What is this all about?"* He was a respectful son, so he was silent along with his father. But as they climb the mountain together, Isaac finally asked, "We have the fire and the wood . . . but where is the sheep for the burnt offering?" (Gen. 22:7) Abraham's answer didn't really solve the mystery rolling around in Isaac's mind. Together they built the altar and spread out the wood. But then it all changed! Can you imagine the confusion, the shock, the terror he felt as his father tied him up and then laid *him* on the altar as the sacrifice or the utter terror he must have felt as Abraham raised his knife intending to kill him? He was about to die at the hand of the father who supposedly loved him! One of the rabbinical stories says that Abraham's face became evil at that moment, as if he had become someone else who was about to kill his son.

When we read the story from Abraham's perspective, it was one of the greatest acts of faith ever recorded. But if we read it from Isaac's point of view, it was a horrible, terrifying act. And because Abraham apparently never talked with Isaac on the way to Mount Moriah, or on the trip back, what had just taken place was still unexplainable.

Then we might ask, what went through Isaac's mind on the way home? Again, the trip home was apparently a three-day journey, *in silence!* If I were Isaac, I would be exploding inside. *"What just went on? How was God part of THAT? I just helped my father build an altar out of wood for a burnt offering. Then this father—the one who says he loves me—ties me up, lifts me to the top of the piled wood, and as I lay there helpless, takes his knife, lifts it high above me, and then stops!* Talk about trauma! We don't know whether Isaac heard the angel cry out to Abraham to stop or not—Abraham just stopped. Then Abraham untied him and noticed a ram caught in the brush. That ram became the sacrifice, but if I had been Isaac, I would have been standing there shaking with the terror of what I had just experienced. *I was almost killed!*

Isaac was still respectful of his father, so on the trip home he waited, hoping his father would explain what had just happened. But Abraham was silent, and in the silence, everything Isaac had believed no longer made any sense. *"What kind of God am I serving?"* he asks himself. *"How could God be a part of this horrible experience? Was my dad actually going to kill me? How could he?"*

When they got home, they couldn't find Sarah, so the answers to Isaac's questions would have to wait; they needed to find Sarah. And then they found that she had died, and Abraham was overwhelmed with grief—no time now for Isaac's questions. In fact, there never was a time for Isaac to find out what that event was all about.

Frederick Buechner has written a novelized version of the story of Isaac. It's entitled *Son of Laughter.*[2] It's a wonderful book that also refers to the traditions of the ancient rabbis. He has a chapter in which he describes Isaac telling his two sons about the experience he and his father had on Mount Moriah. It's a very difficult story for Isaac to relate to his sons; and as he gets close to the end, Buechner describes Isaac as rolling in pain on the ground inside his tent, unable to finish the story. Buechner captures the trauma this event must have caused Isaac. Isaac, like those who have experienced great trauma, retreated inside himself, unable to finish the story. Isaac lived the rest of his life with a huge father wound and, as a result, a wounded relationship with God.

Today, unfortunately, many men are like Isaac. They walk around with a father wound deep inside. Their father may not have traumatized them as Abraham did Isaac, but they've been deeply disappointed in their father's lack of relationship with them. Their father may have been a workaholic, a tyrant, an abuser, an alcoholic, silent or anything else that kept them from being relational with their wives and, especially, with their sons. These fathers were probably wounded sons themselves, so they didn't know anything else but to wound their own children. That father wound carries over into a wounded image of God. Our image of who God is often becomes merged with our experience of what our earthly father was (or is) like.

The Silent Saint

Another generational pattern in Isaac's experience was the favoritism shown by both his father and mother toward him. Isaac was favored over Ishmael, his half-brother, if for no other reason than that Isaac was the child of the promise. He was also born to his mother Sarah in her old age. Abraham's willingness to send Ishmael away, reluctant though he was, also was evidence of his great love and favor toward Isaac.

After Isaac married Rebekah, they also experienced barrenness—20 years with no offspring. This is a repeated theme in Isaac's marriage, as it had been in his parent's marriage. After much pleading with God, finally Rebekah became pregnant—with twins. It wasn't a happy pregnancy, for the twins were fighting with each other in the womb. In despair at one point, Rebekah cried out, "Why is this happening to me?"

I think one of the things Isaac may have vowed soon after he was married was that when he had children no one in his family was going to play favorites with his kids. Think about it. He was maybe four years old when Abraham sent away his brother, Ishmael. Ishmael was about 20 years old at the time. Can you imagine how Isaac viewed his older brother? In Isaac's eyes, his older brother was probably his hero. Most little boys who have an older brother usually idolize that older brother, and maybe Isaac did the same. Apparently there was some ongoing contact between Isaac and Ishmael after Ishmael was sent away; for when Abraham died, they were both there to bury him. But the favoritism of his mother toward Isaac was at the expense of losing his big brother, Ishmael.

But now, as the conflict began in the womb, Isaac's wife, Rebekah, could not understand what was going on inside of her. She inquired of the Lord, and he told her that "the sons in your womb will become two rival nations" (Gen. 25:23). The younger twin would be the child of the promise and would rule over the older twin. So Rebekah made a note of this and wondered what her second-born twin would be like.

When the twins were born, the younger one, Jacob, was trying to hold back the older one by grabbing hold of his heel. And then to complicate everything, Esau, the firstborn, was an "ugly" baby. You know there are ugly babies—but never your own! You've probably had the experience of going to see someone else's baby, and on the way home commented to your spouse, "Wow, that's sure a funny-looking baby—hope he or she changes as she grows." Esau was that kind of baby. He was red all over, and the Bible says, "He was covered with so much hair that one would think he was wearing a piece of clothing" (Gen. 25:25). This was at birth; and apparently from what happened later, his "hairiness" was excessive all of his life.

When twins are born, and you've been told that the younger one is the child of the promise, and he is a beautiful baby, it's easy to understand why Rebekah's heart was immediately drawn toward Jacob. She invested her energy in him, and she "favored Jacob" (v. 28). You can imagine—whenever they went anywhere, Rebekah grabbed Jacob, and Isaac was left to take care of Esau. So over time, Isaac formed a relationship with Esau. In spite of Isaac's vow, Isaac and Rebekah played favorites with their two sons. It's interesting that Abraham and Sarah both favored the same son, whereas Isaac and Rebekah each had their favorite. But the pattern of playing favorites with the children ended up the same in Isaac's family, even though it started out very differently than the favoritism between Isaac and his brother Ishmael.

This favoritism was complicated by Isaac's silence as a father, as a husband and as a man. In most marriages, when there is a silent husband, there is a dominating wife. That's not a criticism of the wife so much as it is of the husband. His lack of involvement leaves a vacuum, so the wife ends up filling the vacuum. She rules the home. That's what Rebekah did.

All of this came into play when Isaac was old and blind and told Esau to go and get him some wild game to eat, for it was time for Esau to receive his father's blessing as the eldest son. Rebekah overheard Isaac telling Esau about the blessing. Rebekah remembered God's words and knew the blessing belonged to Jacob, and apparently she had also been reading the "book of Hezekiah," for she stepped up to help God out of this predicament.

We will never know how God would have worked out this situation if Rebekah had been patient and obedient. But she wasn't; she, like Sarah, solved the problem her way. She called Jacob and told him her plan. He would be disguised as his brother, Esau. She was going to prepare the meal as if it was wild game, and Jacob was to take the meal to Isaac and get the blessing. Jacob protested: "But mother . . . he won't be fooled that easily. Think how hairy Esau is and how smooth my skin is! What if my father touches me? He'll see that I'm trying to trick him, and then he'll curse me instead of blessing me" (Gen. 27:11-12).

Rebekah would have nothing to do with his protest, and said, "Let the curse fall on me, dear son" (v. 13). And then she told him what to do. Jacob was also a mama's boy, so he did what he was told. You know the story—she took the skins of two young goats, made gloves and a collar for Jacob, prepared the food, and sent him in to his father.

As Jacob went in to his father, Isaac asked who it was. Jacob, the deceiver, lied. He told his father that he was Esau. Isaac asked how he found the game so quickly, and Jacob said, "Because the LORD *your* God put it in my path!" (v. 20, emphasis added). Here's only one of the interesting nuances in this story. I would think that Jacob would have said, "the Lord *our* God . . ." But Jacob spoke honestly here. As we see later in the story, Jacob had little or no knowledge of the God of the promise. God was not *his* God, he was his father's God. Part of Isaac's silence precluded any passing on of the knowledge of God, and so any knowledge of God in Jacob was missing, as was the knowledge of the promise of God in both of his sons.

Jacob's response made Isaac suspicious. He wanted his son to come close so he could touch him. As he touched the gloves on his hands, Isaac said to himself, "The voice is Jacob's, but the hands are Esau's" (v. 22). He knew something wasn't right, but he let it slide. It's interesting how in our families we may be aware that there is something going on that isn't quite right, but we ignore it. Isaac ignored his suspicion, probably because he didn't want to make trouble for anyone. But by ignoring his suspicion, he ended up causing even more trouble. As Isaac finished the meal he was still unconvinced, so before Isaac gave the blessing, he asked his son for a kiss. This time the smell of Esau's clothes, which Jacob was wearing, convinced him and he blessed Jacob as the firstborn.

Jacob couldn't wait to get out of there, and soon after he left his father, Esau arrived and found out that his despised brother had robbed him once again. He was angry and vowed to kill Jacob as soon as his father died.

It's important to note here that all families are dysfunctional to some degree. Dysfunction means that something isn't working the way it was designed, and families don't work the way God designed them to work due to sin. Some are more dysfunctional, some less, but all are dysfunctional.

Isaac and Rebekah were the parents of a very dysfunctional family. Here's the result: Esau made a vow to kill Jacob, and perhaps he told a friend who told another friend who told his mother who told Rebekah. Obviously, Rebekah then feared for Jacob's life, so she went to Isaac and came up with a plan to get Jacob far away from home. She told Isaac she wanted to send Jacob to her brothers so he wouldn't marry any of the local women. After all, Esau had married several local women, and they were a real pain-in-the-neck for Rebekah. She didn't want any more local daughters-in-law. And Isaac agreed!

Now, if this had been a healthy family, when Rebekah came to Isaac about Jacob, Isaac would have said, "Wait a minute! We need to talk about what just happened in there with Jacob posing as Esau." But that didn't happen. Once again, Isaac was silent, and Jacob was sent away to his uncle's house.

So What Can We Learn?

Perhaps the sadness in the story of Isaac is that his faith always remained restrained. He never could really trust his father after the "almost sacrifice" on Mount Moriah. As a result, he never could really trust anyone, even the God of his father. So he withdrew into himself. His silence kept him stuck. Since he never fully recovered from his father-wound, he didn't speak of God with his sons. He was the silent father in many ways, but he was especially silent about his faith and his relationship with God. It doesn't mean he lost his faith or turned his back on God. No, he was faithful, but he was silent. The result is that little is said of him in Genesis, and even less is said of him in Hebrews 11, the faith chapter. He is included in the list of saints, but all it says is, "It was by faith that Isaac blessed his two sons, Jacob and Esau. He had confidence in what God was going to do in the future" (Heb. 11:20). That confidence only showed itself in the blessing of his sons.

While a silent father is usually a silent husband, and this has a negative effect on the marriage, the real victims of silent fathers are the children. My mother-in-law grew up with a silent father. He would sit at the dinner table and give a grunt, and the children would panic as they tried to figure out what he wanted. If they gave him the butter when he wanted the salt, he would then rage. No one in the family ever knew what he wanted, what he thought or what he cared about. There was no creative input into his children—he was just an angry, silent presence in the home that the children tried their best to avoid.

In Augusten Burroughs's novel *A Wolf at the Table,* he describes growing up with a silent father who had never wanted him. His father was a shadowy presence—a form on the stairs, a cough from the basement, who eventually became a threat to his safety. He was the wolf at the dinner table. Burroughs writes, "I always found his silence more alarming than his cacophony," referring to the crazy-making games his father played with him over the years.[3]

In Isaac's case, we don't know if he grunted at the dinner table, or how angry he was. We just know he wasn't a factor in the shaping of his sons, especially when it came to their knowledge of God and of the promise. Esau ends up rejecting the God of his father and grandfather, and Jacob leaves home with no understanding of the God he will meet the first night he is away from home. There is little else we can say about Isaac, the silent saint.

The Fearful Saint

Surely the LORD is in this place, and I wasn't even aware of it.
GENESIS 28:16

Jacob is typically considered the "good twin," for obviously, when we compare him to Esau, he comes out looking good. Over the centuries, the rabbis have always seen Esau as an evil man. There was nothing in Esau's life that even hinted at holiness or sainthood, so Jacob benefits by the comparison. But that doesn't really tell us much about Jacob.

I talked with a young man once whose father's name was Jacob. He was not very happy with his father at the time, and he said, "My dad's named well—he's a Jacob—a deceiver, or better yet, he's what we think of when we think of the caricature of a 'used-car salesman.'" The name does tell us something about Jacob, for there is a deceptive, selfish and even ruthless part to his character. Foiled in the birthing process from being the oldest, he tricks his older brother into giving him the birthright in exchange for a bowl of soup, which meant he got two-thirds of the inheritance rather than one-third. Again he is the trickster when he deceives his father to steal the firstborn's blessing from his brother. And later, throughout the 20 years he lived with his Uncle Laban, either he or his uncle was always the trickster.

Like his father, Jacob was a "mama's boy." He was too close to his mother, who from birth made him her favorite. And he seemed to be distant from and afraid of his father, who favored Esau. It can be an interesting phenomenon when parents have two children, either as twins or close in age. Our first two sons were 13 months apart, and for some time, it was as if we had twins. When we went somewhere, Jan would grab the oldest, and I would grab our other son. If we weren't careful, that could easily have led to our playing favorites. We don't think we did, and the evidence seems to be that both older boys have always felt that their youngest brother was the true favorite—of course, we as the parents feel they are entirely wrong about that!

We'll look more at the dynamics of Jacob and Esau's family in the next chapter, but suffice it to say here that they really weren't a saintly family. Rebekah came from a family that included idol worshippers (see Gen. 31:17ff), and Isaac was silent about whatever faith he had. As a result, both Jacob and Esau grew up with little or no knowledge of the God of their grandfather Abraham.

We saw in the last chapter how in the story of the blessing, Isaac questioned Jacob several times as he pretended to be his brother Esau. Isaac seemed to suspect that something was going on. But in spite of his uncertainty, he went along with the deception, apparently afraid to confront the reality of what he suspected. As soon as Jacob left his father, the real Esau arrived, only to find that Jacob, the usurper, had one-upped him once again. In his anger, Esau determined that after his father died, he would kill Jacob.

It was Esau's anger and determination to finally get revenge that sent Jacob off on the journey where he would encounter the God of his grandfather Abraham. Jacob's spiritual life was focused around two key events (and maybe a third) that took place once he left his mother and his home. We don't know how old Jacob was at this point, for the Bible doesn't tell us his age. Jewish tradition suggests that he was between 63 and 77 years old. According to the rabbis, he was older; he was definitely not a young boy leaving his mother's home.

The First Key Event

It was obviously more than a day's journey to his uncle's home, so Jacob had to find a good place to "camp out" for the night. He'd probably never been to summer camp, and in fact, he had probably never even been away from his home, and his mother. Even though he had servants with him, it was still a scary thing. In fact, Jacob was probably afraid simply because he was running away, not just from his brother, but also from his parents and the comfort and safety they provided. Jacob's world was now a place dominated by fear, even terror, loneliness and guilt. One of the Jewish commentators states that "Jacob is also running away from history. He does not want to take responsibility for his life or his world, or to enter either as an active participant. Until now he has lived out his mother's dreams or simply done what she told him."[1]

Jacob was older in chronological age, but he was still a little boy on the inside. And when it came to faith in God, he was like a little baby. God needed Jacob to "grow up" and become a man—the man of the promise. But as long as Jacob stayed in the comfort of being a mama's boy, he wasn't going to become that man. So when it came time to leave home, and fittingly, on the first night, God and Jacob had an encounter in a place one would least expect to find God. And that marked the beginning of his move toward manhood. To Jacob, I'm sure his first reaction to the dream was "what a scary nightmare!" To us who read about it and understand it, it was a miraculous event. God revealed Himself to Jacob and repeated to him the promise first given to his grandfather Abraham. But to Jacob, it was a frightening introduction to the awesome God of his grandfather.

Jacob would learn that God is often present in those unexpected places, and in this unexpected place, God took the initiative to set up the meeting. The meeting took place in a dream, where Jacob could not resist what he was to experience. Rather than dealing with his fears, his loneliness and his guilt over the past, the dream pointed to a very different future for Jacob. And if Jacob was to take seriously what he was experiencing in the dream, it would be the end of his old way of living.

First, we see in his dream what we call a ladder, as described in the campfire song we sing about "Jacob's Ladder." It could have also been a stairway or a ramp. The important thing is that it was a connection between heaven and earth. Up to now, Jacob had lived against the promise. He had lived as a secular man. Heaven was "up there" beyond man's knowledge and interest. But the dream made the point that heaven and earth are not separated places. They are connected in a way that God's angels or messengers go up to heaven and come down to earth. Traffic goes both ways. The image is powerful. Perhaps Jacob, like we so often do, felt that God and heaven were out there somewhere, but too far away to really matter in this life. It was all reserved for the life to come. The image in Jacob's dream challenged that view as he saw heaven and earth connected in this incredible way where the angels were going back and forth doing God's business.

But the most powerful part of the dream was what Jacob heard the Lord God say to him. First, God verbally repeated the promise He made to Abraham and to Jacob. His offspring would be beyond number and they would be a blessing to all the families of the earth. Then God gave Jacob three specific promises that directly confronted his fears. First, God said, "I am with you!" It was a promise of divine presence.

Second, God promised protection wherever Jacob went. And in Jacob's mind, he must have thought of Esau's promise to kill him. It was the promise of Psalm 91:11-12,14-15, where the psalmist says:

> He will order his angels to protect you wherever you go. They will hold you up with their hands so you won't even hurt your foot on a stone. . . . The LORD says, "I will rescue those who love me. I will protect those who trust in my name. When they call on me, I will answer; I will be with them in trouble. I will rescue and honor them."

Third, God promised a homecoming for Jacob (see Gen. 28:15). It would take 20 years, but God would prove to be faithful and bring Jacob back to his home.

The surprise for Jacob is seen in his first response as he awakened. He said, "Surely the LORD is in this place, and I wasn't even aware of it" (v. 16). It's like God said to him, "Surprise!" And the surprise marked the beginning of Jacob's walk of faith. Prior to the dream, God was just someone his dad knew, but about whom Isaac seldom spoke. God was not really a part of Jacob's experience. But now all that had changed. Jacob had suddenly become aware of the fact that no matter where he would go, God would already be there, and that He cared for him and would protect him.

Jacob's next response to the dream was the realization that he had somehow stumbled into the place where God lived. This was a very childlike response. One of the first questions a child will ask about God is "Where does God live?" and Jacob believed he had found at least the doorway to where this God lived. He named the place Bethel, which means the "House of God," and then he set up a stone marker and anointed it with oil, setting it apart as a very holy place. Jacob was beginning a new phase of his life, but we can't get ahead of the story, for the changes in Jacob did not take place suddenly.

After building the monument to the sacredness of that place, and anointing it with oil, Jacob responded to God's threefold promise with an "if." "If God will indeed be with me and protect me on this journey . . . and if I return safely to my father's home, then the Lord will certainly be my God" (vv. 20-21). Jacob the trickster, the deceiver, is now bound to this God who will walk with him as he manipulates and deceives, and is deceived, by his Uncle Laban. Jacob is changing, but Jacob is still Jacob.

The Second Key Event

The story of Jacob between the two key events—the one with the dream and the other 20 years later as he wrestles with the angel by the brook—is a humorous account of Laban first deceiving Jacob, substituting the older sister, Leah, for the one Jacob had bargained for—Rachel. There is an interesting comparison between the two sisters in Genesis 29:17. It says that "Leah had pretty eyes, but Rachel was beautiful in every way, with a lovely face and shapely figure." I would guess from this description that Leah was just average, but the younger sister was stunning. Jacob fell in love with Rachel. And when it was negotiated that Jacob would work for seven years in order to marry Rachel, the text tells us that "Jacob worked seven years to pay for Rachel. But his love for her was so strong that it seemed to him but a few days" (Gen. 29:20)

One of the important lessons Jacob had to learn was to delay gratification. The seven years that he had to wait to get what he wanted was a wonderful growth experience for him, and it seemed as if he experienced it that way. But then the deception by Laban came into play. Perhaps Jacob had too much spiked punch during the wedding festivities and didn't realize that Laban had substituted the average Leah for the ravishing Rachel on the wedding night, and Jacob didn't know it until the next morning. A masterful deception!

On the other hand, Jacob deceived Laban with the breeding of the sheep. After paying for both Leah and Rachel, Jacob said he wanted the speckled, spotted or black ones as his wages. Laban tried to trick him by removing all the male sheep that were speckled, spotted or black, but then Jacob peeled branches so they were striped, and placed them in front of the sheep as they mated. God indirectly blessed this move on Jacob's part, but there is nothing stated in the text as to God telling him to do this, nor about God communicating in any way with Jacob about the problem. In fact, there is nothing spiritually edifying in any of this in-between part of the story of Jacob, nor are there any situations where we see God actively working in Jacob's life.

God's activity with Jacob seemed to be indirect. He allowed Leah, the unfavored wife, to have six sons, a guaranteed way in that culture to win the approval of your husband. But it didn't work for Leah. Rachel was still the favored one. For years, God didn't allow her to have children. Her barrenness was a parallel to the long barrenness of Sarah, and of Rebekah, and drove her to desperation when she demanded of Jacob that he give her children (see Gen. 30:1). Yet, no matter what, Rachel remained Jacob's favorite. Eventually, God opened Rachel's womb and she bore a son—Joseph, who also became the favored son. Only when God told Jacob it was time to return home did God become directly involved again with Jacob.

One has to honor Jacob for his obedience at this point. Remembering his brother's vow to kill him might have just as easily led him to go anywhere except home. But God told him to return home, and he obeyed. It's only after Jacob dealt with Laban one last time on his journey home that Jacob faced the fact that in going home he would encounter his estranged brother, Esau. When the realization hit him, he didn't have a spiritual experience in that his faith was strong and he trusted God with the outcome—at least not at first. He was still Jacob the manipulator and deceiver. He had a plan. He sent messengers to meet up with Esau, and notice what he instructed them to say: "Humble greetings from *your servant* Jacob. Until now I have been living with Uncle Laban, and now I own cattle, donkeys, flocks of sheep and goats, and many servants, both men and women. I have sent these messengers to inform *my lord* of my coming, hoping that you will be friendly to me" (Gen. 32:4-5, emphasis added).

Now Jacob had received the blessing of the oldest son from his father, and the prophecy from God to his mother that he would rule over his brother. That stolen blessing was the main reason Esau intended to kill him. So the careful wording of the message the servants were to deliver to Esau was in essence saying, "You know that blessing thing—it meant nothing. You're the eldest, and I am your servant. I don't care what God intended by that—I'm even calling you 'my lord.' "

This was a patriarchal family system, in which the oldest man ruled the family like a miniature king. When the father died, his oldest son became the king of the family. There was power in this role, and as the firstborn, that role belonged to Esau. But both the promise and the blessing put Jacob in that role. And Jacob, the deceiver, the trickster, was hoping that the careful wording of his greeting to Esau would defuse the situation.

But like so many of our plans that don't include God, Jacob's attempt at manipulating Esau didn't work. The messengers returned to Jacob and told him that Esau was already on his way to meet him, and that he had an army of 400 men with him! Now Jacob was ready for the second powerful event in his relationship with God.

After 20 years of God's faithfulness in his life, Jacob's faith had grown to a place where he held God accountable for His promises. In his prayer, he prayed, "But you promised me" (Gen. 32:12). But he also didn't just pray and then go to bed. He got ready. He did his manipulative part. First, he selected a large number of animals as gifts for Esau. Then he selected two more groups of animals as gifts and sent the three groups in different directions, giving his servants new instructions. Whichever group met Esau, when he asked whose animals they were, they were to answer, "They belong to *your servant Jacob*, but they are a gift for *his master Esau*" (v. 18). He was depending on God, but he was doing everything he could as well. His reasoning was, "Yes, trust God, but do all the manipulating you can to ensure a good outcome!" Then he divided everyone else into two camps and separated the people and the animals, hoping that in the coming battle with Esau at least one part of the family would survive. Looks like he forgot the promises, or he wasn't going to solely depend on God's promise of protection. When finished with all of his preparation, Jacob retired to his tent. Suddenly, a stranger (an angel) appeared in his tent.

I've always wondered why the angel came to wrestle with him. We were talking about this one time in a Bible study, and someone suggested, "What if he was contemplating suicide?" The more we talked, the more that seemed reasonable. After all, one way Jacob could one-up his brother, whom he was convinced was coming to kill him, was to take his own life. "After all, what does it matter whether I die today or tomorrow. At least if I kill myself, Esau won't have the satisfaction of revenge." But heaven was watching as he played with his knife, and quickly an angel was sent to keep him alive.

Imagine the angel coming into the tent and confronting Jacob, the man ruled by fear. He had no time to be afraid, for he was suddenly angry with the intruder. This was only the second time in his life he'd been angry—the other was when Laban tricked him with Leah on the wedding night. People who are ruled by fear seldom feel anger, and Jacob would have been no exception to that, until this night. This intruder, this angel, perhaps shoved Jacob against the wall of the tent. Jacob didn't need this right now. At first he was surprised, but then he became angry and shoved back. And then the battle was on. All night they fought. When Jacob was tired, the angel let up. When Jacob was strong, the angel was strong.

Finally, when it was time for the angel to leave at dawn, he simply touched Jacob's hip, knocking it out of its socket. What Jacob must have felt at that moment—the physical pain! But suddenly there was the realization that he had not been wrestling with a mere man—a man could not have done what had just happened to him.

So Jacob held on to the angel—healthy anger does not let go of the relationship with the other person. And then he asked for a blessing. He wanted a blessing of his own, not something meant for an older brother. The angel asked him his name, and this time Jacob told the truth. He was not Esau, he was the supplanter, the deceiver, the trickster—his name was Jacob. The blessing was that he was given a new name, for, as the angel said, "You have fought with God and with men and have won" (v. 28).

What's so great about a new name, you ask? Well, in the world of Jacob, at that time, your name had special meaning—it defined you. We still believe that in some ways. You can buy a plaque with your name on it, and with a description of what that names means. My name is David—my plaque says "The Beloved." That's what my name means. In addition, in some of the cultures at the time of Jacob, your name had special power as well. If someone knew your real name, they would have power over you, so people kept their real name a secret from outsiders. Think of Jacob. All of his life he had been defined as Jacob—the supplanter, the deceiver, the trickster. Not a very good character reference. But now the angel gave him a new name, a new identity. He was to be "Israel," which meant "God rules, preserves, and protects," just as God had promised him 20 years before.

But why did the angel knock his hip out of place? I think it was a gift to him. Here's Jacob, the dreamer. The battle ends and the angel leaves. Jacob is exhausted and probably falls asleep briefly. Then he suddenly awakens and thinks to himself, *What a nightmare! It was a dream, only a dream after all.* And then he tries to stand up and can't. *It wasn't a dream. It really happened!* Jacob now knew he had been wrestling with God, for he named the place "Peniel (which means 'face of God'), and he said, 'I have seen God face to face, yet my life has been spared'" (v. 30). What an incredible experience—one that he, in the natural, was not supposed to survive!

Every day after that night by the brook, Jacob walked with a limp, and in that woundedness, he had a daily reminder that he had experienced a real encounter with God. He had the proof. He had a new name, but he also had a new limp. And that limp was the proof of his new name. He "had penetrated the mystery of God" as none before him had. But his victory was also a "dangerous, costly mystery in drawing too near and claiming too much."[2] His woundedness reminded him of that truth every day. Once again, "God was in this place," but this time, Jacob/Israel knew it. In the end, Jacob was changed, for Hebrews 11:21 puts it beautifully when it says, "Jacob . . . bowed in worship as he leaned on his staff." Only God is God.

The encounter at the brook gave Jacob a new name; but as you read through the rest of Genesis, the text alternates between referring to him as Jacob and referring to him as Israel. There seems to be no pattern as to which name is used. It's as if Jacob himself couldn't decide whether he was the new man, Israel, or the old man, Jacob. God even told him to go back to where they began, to Bethel, where Jacob had first encountered God. There God affirmed again His promises to Jacob and also affirmed that his name was no longer to be Jacob. God Himself again renamed him Israel.

But he was still Jacob, and that's important to see. After his reconciliation with Esau, he refused Esau's offer of help for the rest of his journey home. Instead, Jacob promised to meet him in Seir later. But instead, Jacob didn't go to Seir as he had promised Esau; instead he went to Shechem. He was still the deceiver. Had he been transformed by his encounter by the brook? In some ways yes, in other ways he was still the same fearful, manipulative man.

So What Can We Learn?

Jacob's failure to fully incorporate into himself the reality of God and His threefold promise to him leaves Jacob as one we might call the "secular saint." He had two major life-changing events in his life (and a third one when God spoke to him once again at Bethel), but the impact of those events didn't seem to change his basic character. He was still the fear-driven manipulator. He had 20 years of experiencing God's hand of blessing on him while with Uncle Laban. God wasn't bothered, apparently, by Jacob's deceptive manipulation of the sheep while they were breeding. He obviously participated with Jacob, for how could Jacob's white-streaked branches affect the speckling or spots on the newly born lambs unless God was somehow in the background as a part of the process? In fact, Jacob was enriched by his deceptions, just as his father had been enriched after lying about Rebekah being his sister, and his grandfather had been enriched after lying about his wife Sarah being his sister—twice!

Jacob was also a passive man. Fear does that to a man, as does having a passive father. That's why Laban could substitute Leah for Rachel, and Jacob not know it until it was too late. He did complain about that one, but Leah was still his wife. He had to work another seven years to pay for Rachel to be his wife, even though they were married a week later. He was also passive as a husband. For example, his four wives argued with each other as to which one would get to sleep with him on any given night (see Gen. 30:14-18).

He was also a passive father. When the prince of Shechem raped his daughter Dinah, he did nothing. And when his sons destroyed

the men of Shechem, plundering all of their wealth and then taking the women and children to sell into slavery—all in revenge for
what the prince had done to their sister Dinah—Jacob did nothing
except to confront his sons after the fact, saying, "You have ruined
me! You've made me stink among all the people of this land—
among all the Canaanites and Perizzites. We are so few that they
will join forces and crush us. I will be ruined, and my entire household will be wiped out!" (Gen. 34:30). He's at least worried about
the repercussions, but he backed down on this issue when his sons
responded with anger.

Later, after his sons sell their brother Joseph into slavery, the
brothers bring Joseph's coat covered with blood back to Jacob.
When Jacob sees it, he simply accepts the fact that Joseph is dead.
I've wondered why he didn't question his sons as to the exact loca-
tion where they found the coat, and then go there with his servants to begin to search for whatever might be left of Joseph. But
he was too passive to do that.

As a father, he knew how the favoritism of his parents had led
to his having to leave the home, yet he played favorites with both
his wives and his children. When their land was in famine and his
10 sons returned from Egypt with grain, but also with instructions
to bring Benjamin with them when they came back to Egypt, Jacob
was too fearful to let Benjamin go. Benjamin had replaced Joseph
as his favorite son. It wasn't until Judah pointed out that they
would all die if they didn't go back and take Benjamin with them
that Jacob reluctantly allowed him to go. He was too fearful to
really make the changes he probably longed to make in his life.

Perhaps the clearest picture of Jacob's limited faith was in his
failure to be truly reconciled with his brother, Esau. He didn't want
Esau's help in the final part of the journey. In fact, he didn't want
anything to do with Esau, even though it appears that Esau was
genuinely willing to be reconciled with Jacob. According to 1 John
4:20 the proof of our love of God is that we love our brother, for
John says, "If we don't love people we can see, how can we love
God, whom we cannot see?" Of course, one could say that Jacob
must have loved his brother, he just didn't want anything to do

with him. He just didn't like him. But it is far more likely that the growth in his relationship with God during the 20 years with Uncle Laban, and beyond, just didn't penetrate that deeply into his character. Even the rabbis point out that there is little evidence of a deepening faith in Jacob, largely evidenced by his fearful approach to life and his passivity. Jacob never really totally lived for the promise. He was too secular for that.

Jacob's story is a story of a life characterized by fear and the consequence of conflict. Everywhere he goes he is in conflict. It even began in the womb. Then during the growing up years, he is in constant conflict with Esau. When he leaves home, he ends up in ongoing conflict with Laban and his sons. He lives with four wives who are in conflict over him, and sometimes in conflict with him. He is in conflict with 10 of his sons. He is even in conflict with God at times. Yet, in the midst of all the conflict, God is at work in the development of Jacob's knowledge and awareness of Himself. And interestingly, it seems that it is God's commitment to Jacob that is at the root of most of his fears and his conflicts. God sets in motion the conflicts with his choice of Jacob to be the child of the promise (see Gen. 25:23).

I've often seen that the commitment to walking with God creates conflict both within and with others, for we now have a spiritual reality to deal with that is in conflict with much of what is the material reality. Living for the promise is in conflict with everyday life. And this conflict seemed to be at the root of much of Jacob's conflicts, for he could not decide if he was really the child of the promise—Israel—or the secular man, the trickster Jacob.

While God cared that Jacob understood the promise, Jacob seemed more concerned about his accumulation of wealth and sons. The focus on offspring is understandable, as that was a part of the promise given to him. But he was a fearful secular saint in that he was preoccupied with prosperity. How modern was Jacob! God was trying to get his attention, but Jacob was concerned about how many sheep—a measure of wealth—were going to be his.

Another important lesson we can learn from Jacob is that it isn't the profound encounters with God that cause the deepening of our faith walk. We don't move from holey to wholly to holy by a series of wonder-filled encounters with God. It takes much more. We have to internalize and live out what we learn in those encounters. Jacob didn't seem to reflect on the meaning of those encounters in between each event. Perhaps that is why God asked for that third encounter. He was still trying to get Jacob's undivided attention.

Yet in all of this, Jacob was still loved by God, and he was even honored by God. It is a powerful picture of God's grace and love in that He chooses to call Himself "the God of Abraham, of Isaac, and of Jacob." God is proud to be known as the God of that fear-filled trickster named Jacob. He didn't say, "I am the God of Abraham, of Isaac, and of that changed man Israel." God always identifies more with us in those broken places. In fact, "there are no troubled dimensions of human interaction which are removed from the coming of the Holy God."[3]

The Family Dynamics of

*I do not excuse the guilty. I lay the sins of the parents upon their
children and grandchildren; the entire family is affected—
even children in the third and fourth generations.*

EXODUS 34:7

I was raised in a dysfunctional family, and my wife and I created a
dysfunctional family of our own. Now we watch our sons create
their own dysfunctional families. That may sound disrespectful
to some, but once we understand what dysfunctional is, we can
see that there is no disrespect intended. All families are dysfunctional to some extent, because all people are dysfunctional. No one
functions fully as a human was intended to function, for as the
Bible says so clearly, "all have sinned" (Rom. 3:23). The original
design God had when he created mankind was broken by sin, so
everything we touch or are a part of is in some way less than intended. That's what makes it dysfunctional.

You might even go so far as to say that it is redundant to say
"dysfunctional family" since all families are this way, even those
in the Bible. What I appreciate about the families described in
Genesis is that we get an honest picture of four generations of a

dysfunctional family that in each generation becomes increasingly unhealthy. God doesn't "clean up" their story when it's recorded in the Bible, making them saintly, or perfect. No, instead He lets us see them as real people with hang-ups, relational deficiencies and other problems.

The passage in Exodus 34:7 tells us that the dysfunctional patterns of the parents are passed on for three or four generations. At that point, the problems have probably increased in their unhealthiness to a point where someone stops the pattern only to have other patterns continue on their three- to four-generational course. It is interesting that the Bible makes this point. In the study of how families work, which began after World War II, the researchers found that all families had their problem patterns, or what was later called generational patterns, and that these patterns would continue for three or four generations until someone put a stop to that particular pattern. Sounds just like what the Bible had already told us!

The family of Abraham and Sarah is where the family stories in Genesis begin; although we get a little information about Abraham and Sarah's parents, we don't get enough to understand how they behaved. We do have enough information about Abraham and Sarah. We've already commented in earlier chapters on the pattern of lying that Abraham and Sarah used on at least two occasions—saying that Sarah was Abraham's sister. And how Isaac and Rebekah repeated that pattern at least once. The pattern seems to stop there; so maybe Abraham's father, Terah, did something similar with his wife.

The pattern that seems to begin with Abraham was that of the favoritism the parents played with their sons. In Abraham's immediate family, both Abraham and Sarah favored Isaac over Ishmael. The consequence of their favoritism was that one of the sons was sent away. If this is a generational pattern, then we will see the same thing in Isaac's family, and we do. In Isaac's family, the pattern began in a somewhat different way. They had twins, and the parents each had a favorite, as opposed to Abraham and Sarah favoring the same son. But the ending was the same. One son was eventually sent away. Jacob was sent away to live with Uncle Laban.

When we look at the third generation, Jacob's family began differently as well. He had two wives, and he played favorites with his wives. The result was that he would favor the child of Rachel, his favorite wife, and then both he and Rachel did it as well; they had a favorite son named Joseph. We'll see in the next chapter how he was favored and how the generational consequence again was that one of the sons—Joseph—was sent away. The pattern of favoritism with a son being sent away stops with Joseph, the fourth generation. It's just as God said it would be in Exodus 34:7.

Notice also the increased seriousness of the problem that causes each son to be sent away. In the first generation, Ishmael was sent away basically due to Sarah's jealousy and over-protection of Isaac. In the next generation, Jacob was sent away because his brother wanted to kill him. In the third generation, Joseph was sent away after most of his brothers were fully intent on killing him and even had the opportunity to do the deed. That's what happens over the years with these generational patterns—they become increasingly destructive. What we want to look at, though, is what we can learn from the dynamics of the families in Genesis that to some degree and in some way occur in every family.

Isaac and Rebekah's Family Dynamics

We said earlier that perhaps Isaac made a vow when he got married that when he had children there would be no playing of favorites. But vows never work. The dynamics of the family patterns are simply too strong. When my first son was born, I vowed I would be a different father to him than my father was to me. About the time my oldest was graduating from high school, to my dismay I realized that my vow hadn't worked. Although I had done all kinds of things with my sons that my father had never done with me, the quality of our relationship wasn't really any different than what I had experienced with my father. It took something more to break the generational pattern.[1]

So how was the pattern carried on in Isaac's family? We don't know the specifics, but perhaps it was simply the dynamics of having twins that helped set in motion the pattern of favoritism in Isaac's family. There were probably other factors as well, such as the knowledge that Rebekah had that Jacob would someday rule over Esau and that he was to be the child of the promise. As the boys grew, the favoritism developed to the point where we read that "Isaac loved Esau because he enjoyed eating the wild game Esau brought home, but Rebekah loved Jacob" (Gen. 25:28).

Another pattern was that both Isaac and Jacob were mama's boys. As a result, the favoritism was intensified. Jacob probably loved to hang around the tent. He learned to cook. He must have been a good cook, for he sold a cup of soup to his brother for a third of the inheritance—probably the most expensive bowl of soup ever. He probably liked to clean the tent and do other "female" chores. Over time, he was probably considered a "sissy" in his father's eyes.

Esau, on the other hand, sounded like a man's man. He loved to hunt and fish. Probably never took a bath, and certainly never used deodorant. That's why when Jacob wore Esau's clothes when he deceived his father, he smelled like Esau. Wherever Isaac went, that's where Esau went. And wherever Rebekah went, that's where Jacob went. You can see that over time there was a tight relationship that developed between Mom and Jacob, and between Dad and Esau. Eventually, Isaac had little to do with Jacob, just as Rebekah had little to do with Esau.

How Early Experiences Shape Us

What did Jacob and Esau miss in their early development based on the family dynamics of favoritism? We have a wonderful opportunity to see this because the parents were so split in their favoritism. And what we see in these two boys can help us understand some important dynamics in our own experiences. To do this, we need to look at the patterns and needs of our early development—during our first two or three years of life. I took classes on this subject, but

I didn't really understand it thoroughly until I was able to observe this process in my grandchildren.

Life begins prior to birth, and that part of our lives is totally dependent on the mother. When the fetus is in the womb, he or she is literally connected to Mom. The mom's voice, moods and emotions, choices of foods, upset stomachs—both the mom and the fetus experience all of these together. He or she also hears Dad's voice as well as other voices in the family, but none as often as Mom's. So when the fetus passes through the birth canal, it's like he or she is looking around to see to whom that voice belongs. There's a reason why that new infant wants to find Mom.

I watched as my grandson was taken from his mom and dad soon after he was born. The nurse brought him by for us to see. He was messy, but beautiful. After all, he was our grandson! Then the nurse took him into the nursery at the hospital. They put him on a table and turned on bright lights and then proceeded to "scrape" him clean. Now I know they were very gentle with him, but nothing had ever touched him before, and I wanted them to be even gentler. And the bright lights—please, this baby has been in complete darkness for nine months. Then they stretched him so they could measure him. Then they took footprints. And then they put some stuff in his eyes—all while he screamed and cried. Then they finally wrapped him and put him in a bassinet, and he went to sleep. Quite a welcome to this new world!

When he woke up, it was a different world from the womb. Back in the womb, everything was tempered, such as sounds and temperature. And it was a world where there were no felt needs. Never hungry, never deficient in vitamins and minerals—a perfect world just like the Garden of Eden. But now he was in an imperfect world, and for the first time he experienced a need—he was hungry. At the time, I thought breast-feeding was natural, but both he and his mom had to learn how to successfully transfer the food from her to him. Mom even had a coach come to the hospital and show her some of the "tricks" of breast-feeding. I thought about this afterward and realized that was probably why babies lose weight the first couple of days. They have to learn how to eat, either from the breast or from the bottle.

Now think about the first task my grandson was facing. He had moved from the perfect environment to a very imperfect environment. And he had no way to communicate specific needs, although eventually moms can tell what a cry is about—whether it is a "diaper is burning" cry, or "I'm hungry" kind of cry. But that comes later. His immediate need at birth is to somehow make this imperfect world seem safe. Mom is the best candidate to help him feel safe, since he already knows her.

So the primary task is to reconnect quickly with Mom; and the way he is going to do that is through the emotion of love. That's why your baby is always the most beautiful baby and so easy to love. God designed it that way so that the mother and baby can quickly reconnect. And even though there are a myriad of things the baby is going to experience, the primary task during the first six to eight months of a baby's life is to feel connected and safe.

I have three sons and no daughters. So when my first grandchild turned out to be a little girl, I was committed to become an important person in her life. I was going to form an attachment with her and be one of those people who made the world safe for her. So every chance I had I would hold her, talk baby talk with her, cuddle with her and put her on my shoulder, hoping that she would go to sleep. When her mom wanted to put her in the crib, I said, "No, let her stay right here." And I would hold her while she slept until she woke up. Babies are so cuddly when they wake up, at least for a short time. Then when she started to cry, I would give her to her mom. That's the privilege of being a grandparent.

About the seventh or eighth month, I was soon to experience the second important task in development. Suddenly my granddaughter wasn't very happy when I would hold her. She would squirm and want down. Or if I tried to hold her close, she would push me away. I was bothered by this, thinking she was upset with me. Then I realized that she now felt safe enough that she wanted to explore more of her world. She was tired of my neck. So I'd put her down, and eventually she learned to crawl and then to walk.

Isn't it interesting that when babies start to crawl, and then walk, they are always going away from Mom or whoever was holding them. That's the purpose of this second phase of development. They want to see what else or who else is out there. They want to explore this new world. And here is where Dads are so important. When the toddler wants to walk or crawl away from Mom, she needs to have a safe relationship with Dad so she can go to him. And from him, she will hopefully learn how to channel the aggressive or angry parts of her emotions, as they develop, in appropriate ways.

First we have the movement toward Mom and other significant people that is motivated by the emotion of love. Second, we have the movement away from Mom and others in order to explore the world. The emotion that motivates that movement away we will call the "energy of anger." Dad does a lot to teach his son or daughter about how to handle anger. The "terrible twos" are called that because a child has learned to say no, and anger has become a part of his or her emotional repertoire. A "good-enough" dad will teach his child how to contain that anger, both by example and by the way he responds to his child's anger.

For example, let's say that little Mary is having a very bad "mommy day." Nothing goes right for either Mary or her mom. By the time Dad comes home, Mom is exhausted and Mary is totally frustrated and frustrating. As Dad comes through the door, Mary runs to him with open arms. Dad knows nothing about the day, so he asks Mary, "How was your day?" She says, "Bad day. Mommy mean! I hate Mommy!" Now this dad is wise. As he holds her close, he just listens and keeps Mary talking, telling him about all the "bad things Mommy did" today. As he walks into the family room, he sees Mom stretched out on the couch. She hasn't even had time to comb her hair, it's been that kind of day. Dad wisely heads for the couch as he holds Mary and listens, and then sits down by Mom. Soon Mary is done with her review of the terrible day, and after a few minutes of silence, her next words will be "I want Mommy."

What did Dad just do as he held Mary and listened to her? He contained Mary's anger, making it safe for her to feel the anger without doing anything hurtful to either Mommy or herself. Once the anger was acknowledged, Mary wasn't angry anymore, and now she wanted Mommy. That's how a parental team should work in that situation. So Mom is the primary teacher of love, and Dad is the primary teacher about anger.

We've talked about two emotions: love and anger. Love is the emotion of attachment and is experienced primarily through the mother (or the mothering person). Anger is the emotion of separation. We set our boundaries through the energy of anger, and Dad is the person who is supposed to teach us how to manage our anger in healthy ways. Love, as shown to us by Mom, is the way we learn to say yes to life. Anger, as managed by Dad, is the way we learn to say no to things in life. A healthy balance of having enough from Mom and enough from Dad helps us learn how to have healthy relationships and how to set proper limits in our relationships. (Of course, there are some situations where Dad becomes the "mothering figure" and Mom may become the "fathering figure." But we are talking about generalities here.)

Developmentally, there is a third important emotion, and it is fear. Healthy fear keeps us away from danger. But fear is also just sitting there waiting in the shadows to fill in any gaps in what we are experiencing in love from our mom, or in learning from our dad how to manage our anger and aggressiveness. Fear is the opposite of both love and anger in that it is a withdrawal response rather than a connecting emotion. Therefore, when we have deficits in our ability to love, or in our ability to express anger in healthy ways, we find that fear fills in the gap. Our love is in conflict with our fear, and/or our freedom to be angry in appropriate ways is in conflict with our fear.

So let's look at how these three developmental emotions were experienced in Isaac and Rebekah's family. We can see how this operates in this family because the favoritism of the parents isolated, to a great degree, the desired emotional effect of the other parent. Let's look first at Jacob. We see Jacob as having a lot of his mother's attention and very little of his father's attention. So he learned how to love from his relationship with his mother, but he didn't learn much about anger and setting boundaries from his relationship with his father. Fear then filled in the gap of his lack of learning about healthy anger from his father. As a result, he ended up as a man who knew how to love but didn't know how to set appropriate limits. He didn't know how to say no directly. His love was filled with fear.

Does that explanation fit the image of Jacob we find in Scripture? Yes. He was a lover. He had good relationships with his wives, but he didn't know how to say no to anyone. So to make up for his inability to say no, he used manipulation. Let's look at a contemporary Jacob—someone you might know—who is asked to come to the church on Saturday to help in a "clean-up day." Our contemporary Jacob doesn't know how to say no either. He doesn't really want to participate, and he had other things planned for Saturday, but he couldn't say no to whoever asked him. But, on Friday night, he calls the person who asked him and begs off on the clean-up day because he is feeling sick. He couldn't say no directly, so he has to manipulate the situation.

Jacob's ability to love was also limited by his fear. After growing up with a smothering mother, he welcomed the fact that he had to divide himself between his wives. Rachel had most of him, but not all of him, so she couldn't smother him; but then neither could any of the other wives. He's like the man I met early in my counseling practice and who always had to have an affair going on because he was afraid to really commit all of himself to his wife.

What about Esau? He experienced something from his relationship with his father, but very little from his mother. So his capacity to love was never really developed. He really didn't get much from his dad either since, as we've seen in an earlier chapter, Isaac was a silent father. But Esau could express his anger. It's just that the expression of his anger typically wasn't a healthy use of anger because it was also mixed with fear. Again, fear filled in where love was missing. Anger, when mixed with fear, is a defensive type of anger designed to keep people away from any meaningful encounter in a relationship. It's like those who walk around all the time with a chip on their shoulder so that people keep their distance from them.

Does this fit the Esau we meet in Scripture? Yes. He is obviously an angry man who trusts no one. And why shouldn't he be angry? His brother had stolen the firstborn's blessing and earlier had shown no compassion, requiring an extra third of the inheritance as payment for a bowl of soup. His mother avoided him. But is his anger expressed in a healthy way? Hardly. He is so angry with his brother that he is determined to kill him. And then 20 years later, he comes to his meeting with Jacob, prepared to do battle, with an army of 400.

What about his relationships? He apparently had several wives whom he basically ignored and who were a real problem for his mother, Rebekah. After Jacob stole the blessing of the eldest from him, Esau overheard Mom and Dad talking about sending Jacob away, because as Rebekah said, I'm "sick and tired of these local Hittite women! I would rather die than see Jacob marry one of them" (Gen. 27:46). So what did Esau do? He went out and "married one of Ishmael's daughters, in addition to the wives he already had" (Gen. 28:9). It was as if he were saying, "In your face, Mom and Dad." His latest marriage was a very angry statement.

How would you like to have been that new wife? "So why did your husband marry you?" you might ask her. And if she knew the truth, she would have to say, "To get back at his parents." Not a great reason to marry, and not a good foundation for a healthy relationship. From what we know about Esau, he was not a relational man. He was just an angry man who also operated out of his fear.

So What Can We Learn?

All of us have either a little bit of Jacob in us, or a little bit of Esau in us. We didn't get enough of mom, so our ability to love is mixed with a lot of fear. Or we didn't get much of dad, so our anger is out of bounds, designed to keep people from getting too close to us; or we take the passive role in our relationships and hide our anger and hurt. Are we anger-based in our relationships? Not enough dad, and probably not enough mom either. Or is our ability to love always mixed with fear in our relationships? Probably not enough mom in the early growing-up years.

We see this in operation in the next generation of Jacob's family, when 10 of Jacob's sons never got much of Dad because he was so preoccupied with Rachel. We see it in their anger with their brother Joseph, which grew to the point where they were willing to murder him. And we see it in their anger at the people of Shechem when they killed all the men and sold the women and children into slavery. Their angry act of revenge was way out of bounds and was the result of their inability to manage their anger in healthy ways, probably because they never got much of Dad.

When we look at Joseph, in the next chapter, we'll see another pattern that is the result of having too much of his dad and too much of his mom. We'll see what that does in the early developmental years. Isn't it great that these biblical families had so many problems? How like us they were!

The Victimized Saint

And we know that God causes everything to work together for the good of
those who love God and are called according to his purpose for them.
ROMANS 8:28

Steve Jobs, in a commencement address several years ago, talked about connecting the dots in our life. He made the point that it is a task that can only be done by looking back in time, not looking forward. As an example, he told about how he and a friend had started Apple Computers in his parents' garage, when he was 20. Over the next 10 years, Apple grew to be a $2 billion company with more than 4,000 employees. At that point in time, the board of directors of the company Jobs had started fired him. Jobs said it was the most devastating thing that ever happened to him. But rather than give in to the despair, he decided that based on what he loved to do, he would start a new company. And then he started a second company. These two companies are NeXT, and Pixar Animation, which produced the movie *Toy Story* and a host of other animated movies and features. With no thought of Apple, Jobs poured himself into his new ventures and enjoyed his renewed creativity.

Some years later, Apple bought NeXT, and as a result, Jobs returned to Apple Computers. Because of his new role at Apple, we now have the iPod, the iPhone, the iPad, and who knows what else, because Steve Jobs returned to Apple. He said that when he was let go at the age of 30, he could have figured that his dream was destroyed. But not knowing anything about the future, he simply jumped in again and did what he loved. It was only in looking backwards in time that he could see how the pieces were all connected.

The story of Joseph is the archetype of this type of situation. If Joseph had looked forward in time, everything would have appeared to be lost. He was separated from his family and sold into slavery. And then, even though he did his best, he was falsely accused and thrown into an Egyptian prison for years. Where does one find hope in that? Joseph trusted God each step of the way, but it was only in looking back near the end of the story that he could clearly see God's hand in everything that occurred in his life. Through his connecting the dots later in life, he could say to his brothers, "You intended to harm me, but God intended it all for good" (Gen. 50:20).

Joseph is a powerful figure in the book of Genesis, and he represents the fourth generation we meet in Abraham's family. He is the one who will be the transformational figure in the family's dysfunctional patterns we've already talked about. Favoritism will stop with his family, but only after he bears the brunt of the generational patterns and is almost murdered by his brothers. He is the third son in three generations to be sent away from home. In his case, his being sold into slavery was a much better option than being murdered. The pattern began with Ishmael, when he was sent away because Sarah was jealous. In the next generation, Jacob was sent away because his mother was fearful that he would be murdered. Now, in this generation, Joseph is almost murdered, but then is sent away by being sold into slavery. Only the protective hand of God kept him alive.

Hollywood has been fascinated with the story of Joseph. The musical play that focuses on his coat of many colors is fairly accurate to the biblical story, and it is great entertainment. So are the several animated versions, such as *Prince of Egypt*, which have been produced. I especially enjoyed watching one of the animated versions because it seemed to really show the pain and suffering Joseph must have experienced as he languished in prison as an innocent man.

Most of the sermons I remember hearing about Joseph's life have focused more on the end of Joseph's story—about how Joseph's dreams became a reality. As the prime minister of Egypt his brothers bowed down low before him out of respect for his position as the second most powerful man in Egypt at that time. Or sermons have focused on his faithfulness to God as Potiphar's wife desperately sought to seduce him. His moral character is rightly held up as a shining example for all of us.

In much that has been said and written about Joseph, he is portrayed as an early type of Christ. His life mirrored Jesus'. What Jesus experienced in becoming human—his rejection and betrayal—is mirrored in Joseph's rejection by his brothers and their betrayal of him. Jesus was brought low in the crucifixion and his death. Joseph was brought low in his enslavement and imprisonment. In the resurrection and at the end of time, we see Jesus in His ultimate exaltation by God the Father. In a similar way, Joseph ends up exalted as the second most powerful man in the known world at that time. Joseph was sold for 20 pieces of silver; Jesus was betrayed for 30 pieces of silver. Jesus brought spiritual salvation from the slavery of sin, whereas Joseph brought physical salvation from slavery to those who had betrayed and rejected him—even hated him. Like Jesus, he forgave those who, at least in their intentions, wanted to put him to death. And like it is with Jesus, all had to come to him for relief, or perish.

At the same time, Joseph's story, like that of Abraham's, Isaac's, and Jacob's before him, is filled with deceptions and false accusations. He is still part of that increasingly unhealthy family of Abraham, Isaac, and Jacob. As a boy, Joseph would tattle on his brothers, probably exaggerating the tale to make his brothers look bad. Whether true or not, his tattling only added to their hatred of him. He was falsely accused of raping Potiphar's wife, and he falsely accused his brothers of being spies. He deceived his brothers several times, including younger brother Benjamin; and of course, his brothers lied for years to their father Jacob about the fate of Joseph. What a family!

I've often wondered what dinner might have been like in Jacob's home after Joseph was presumed dead. Rachel had died; and Bildah and Zilpah, Jacob's other two wives, are not mentioned and presumably are dead at the time. Only Leah was left as a wife for Jacob. Suppose you are a traveler who has been invited as a guest to their home for dinner. The patriarch of the family is deeply depressed and quiet. Long after Joseph was gone, he was still grieving even though the tradition in the Jewish culture is that you only grieve for a year.

The only daughter, Dinah, probably helped Leah with the meal, and there are 11 sons sitting around the table. One is young and sits next to his father. You can feel the tension in the home. You watch the other 10 sons and notice that they are being hypervigilant with each other. You don't know why, but we do. They had a secret and they had to carefully watch each other so that no one might let a sliver of the secret slip out. Families are as sick as their secrets, and Joseph's family had a massive secret. They watch as Dad grieves for Joseph, believing he is dead; but they know Joseph may still be alive, probably somewhere in Egypt. Again, what a family! But they are also part of the biblical record. Their story is in the Bible!

What We Often Overlook

Not much time is spent on understanding the young adolescent Joseph, neither by the commentators nor by the Jewish rabbis. But that's an important part of the story. It tells us why his brothers hated him so much. No one likes a tattler, and "Joseph reported to his father some of the bad things his brothers were doing" (Gen. 37:2) while out in the fields tending the sheep. But the bigger issue was that "Jacob loved Joseph more than any of his other children" (v. 3). It was a natural consequence of Jacob favoring Joseph's mother, Rachel; but as the verse adds, it was also because "Joseph had been born to him in his old age."

Unlike his father, Jacob, who was favored only by his mother, both Joseph's father and mother loved him, and both doted on him. He got so much attention that it is easy to see why he felt so entitled, so self-centered, so grandiose and was, at the same time, so naive. Whereas his father Jacob was sneaky, Joseph was right out there, and as a result, could be called "insufferable!" At 17, it's easy to understand his being selfish—most adolescents are. But the entitlement, the grandiosity, coupled with the naiveté made him an obnoxious brat in the family. Trust me, if he'd been your brother, you'd have hated him as well.

Imagine breakfast. Joseph comes to the table, and maybe Dad asks, "Any dreams last night?" And Joseph tells him about a dream in which he and his brothers are in the field tying up bundles of grain: "Suddenly my bundle stood up, and your bundles all gathered around and bowed low before mine!" (v. 7).

Now remember, we know the end of the story. Joseph's brothers did not. To the brothers, this was just another arrogant dream by their pampered brother, which only added to their hatred of him. Then, one morning, Joseph had another dream, and this one included his father and mother. Here was an example of his naiveté—he told his dreams to his brothers, as if they cared. But in this dream, he said, "The sun, moon, and eleven stars bowed low before me" (v. 9), which included Mom, who was apparently the moon, and Dad, who was apparently the sun. This time, even his father protests a little, and later on, Jacob wondered what the dream was all about.

Now, not only is Joseph naive about his brothers' feelings toward him, but apparently his dad is also unaware of what's going on in the family. Joseph has a new coat. I like to imagine that his dad bought it for him at Neiman Marcus, while the rest of the boys got their clothes at the Salvation Army Thrift Store. This coat was more than beautiful. According to the stories of the rabbis, it apparently had some regal significance by the way it was made and the cloth from which it was made. Jacob suggested that Joseph go and check on his brothers, and perhaps added, "And wear your new coat so they can see it."

Now, if I was Joseph, and I knew what my brothers felt about me, I would have done the minimum expected of me. For starters, I wouldn't have worn the coat. And when I got to Shechem, where they were supposed to be, and they were not there, I would have returned home. But no, not Joseph. He checked around to find out where they had gone, and when told they had relocated to Dothan, he continued on another day's journey to Dothan to find his brothers.

I imagine that as he approached from the distance, one of the brothers said to the others, "If he tells me another dream, I'll literally kill him!" Then another adds, "Well, why do we need another dream? Let's just kill him, and then we'll see what becomes of his dreams." They proceed to take his coat from him and then throw him into a dry well—a cistern. The rabbis added that the cistern was filled with snakes and scorpions, but also said the Lord didn't allow them to bite him.

While Joseph is yelling at his brothers to stop, perhaps adding, "It's not funny anymore!" his brothers sit down to eat and discuss how they are going to kill Joseph. As they talk (and Joseph can hear their deliberations), they see some Ishmaelite traders heading to Egypt, and Judah suggests that instead of having his blood on their hands, they sell him into slavery. So they did. In their effort to "clean up" the behavior of these future "heads of the tribes of Israel," the rabbinical stories show the brothers having second thoughts about what they had done. They chased after the Ishmaelite traders to get Joseph back, but they couldn't find them. So they went back to their original plan.

They dipped Joseph's robe into a young goat's blood with the intention of deceiving their father, suggesting that some wild animal had killed Joseph. I've always wondered why Jacob accepted their report. If I had been Jacob, I would have gathered all my servants, and my sons, and said, "Tell me exactly where you found this." Then I would have searched and searched, hoping that I could at least find something I could bury. When I read the rabbis' description of this part of the story, they suggest the same thing, adding that they were to capture any wild animal they found to see if it was the "murderer."

Joseph, the Ultimate Victim

Let's go back to Joseph. Over the years, as a family counselor, I've heard a lot of horrible stories of people being victimized by family members. But I don't think I've ever heard one that tops Joseph's story in terms of unfairness. To me, Joseph is the ultimate victim. Here's why. First, he was hated by his brothers, and in his naiveté, he had no idea why they hated him. They hated him so much that this biblical family of brothers almost murdered one of their own. Second, he was a free man who had now become a slave. He had lost his freedom! Third, he was taken to a strange land, with a strange language and different customs, where he ended up being sold to an Egyptian man named Potiphar, who was the captain of the palace guard.

Now that may not sound so bad, until we understand what some of Potiphar's duties were. As the captain of the palace guard, he was also Pharaoh's chief executioner. How would you like him to be your new owner? Tradition also suggests that someone this high up in Pharaoh's administration was probably also a eunuch. He had a "wife" for ceremonial purposes, but she wasn't really his wife in a wifely way.

Now all of this took place when Joseph was 17. He was still very young. But like many people who have been victimized, they overcompensate, and Joseph certainly did. Instead of simply giving up and living for himself, he became the best slave in Potiphar's household and soon was given responsibility for everything in Potiphar's household. This is a testimony to the developing moral and spiritual character of Joseph, for as the Genesis record twice says, "The LORD was with Joseph" (see Gen. 39:2,23). He didn't just give up; he rose above it! Now let's say it took him several years to earn Potiphar's favor, and during that time, he became a very attractive man and drew Potiphar's wife's attention to the point that she lustfully desired to sleep with him.

The rabbis said Potiphar's wife's name was Zuleika. Perhaps since she was a ceremonial "wife," she could sleep with whomever she wanted, as long as she was discreet about it. But we see in this not only Joseph's development of character but also his growing relationship with God. He refuses her advances, ends up being falsely accused of rape—another injustice on top of all the others—and he is put in prison. Why didn't Potiphar just cut off his head? Perhaps he knew his wife was lying, but he had to do something. So once again, Joseph is the victim, and once again, he rises above it all and becomes the best and most trusted prisoner in the palace jail. None of this is what Joseph wanted for his life. But he never gave in to the injustices, the unfairness of it all.

Don't get ahead of the story or you will miss the pain and injustice Joseph experiences along the way. Nothing goes right! And now he is in prison and seemingly forgotten by everyone. How long was he in prison? We don't know exactly. But let's say it took a couple of years to rise to the top as Potiphar's most trusted servant. So maybe he hits 21 or 22 when Zuleika accuses him of rape. That means he was in prison for eight or nine years. Forgotten! It must have felt that way, although the rabbis have suggested that Zuleika even pursued him while he was in prison.

Why so long in prison? The Bible doesn't tell us. I've always looked at his prison days as his "recovery program"—a time for healing. Think about the resentments, the hurts, and the rejection he's experienced. As he sat alone in prison, he had a lot of time to reflect on the past. Gradually, perhaps in conversations with other prisoners, he began to understand how he'd been set up. He wondered why his brothers hated him so much. Eventually, he saw how the favoritism of his parents set the stage for that hatred. He still didn't understand the purpose of it all—only later would he see that. He just needed to see the destructive patterns in his life and in his family that had led him to this place. He began to see and understand, and as a result, he turned his prison into the place of healing.

Then, when he was 28, he interpreted the dreams of the palace baker and the palace wine taster. He told the baker that in three days he would lose his head to Pharaoh's sword. He told the wine taster that in three days he would be released from prison and restored to his job. Then he made an important request. He asked the wine taster to, "Please remember me and do me a favor when things go well for you. Mention me to Pharaoh, so he might let me out of this place" (Gen. 40:14). Then he added, "For I was kidnapped from my homeland, the land of the Hebrews, and now I'm here in prison, but I did nothing to deserve it" (v. 15). Then the ultimate disappointment—the wine taster forgot about Joseph for two years!

Why two more years in prison? I think God wasn't finished with him yet. The book of Proverbs 30:21 tells us there "are three things that make the earth tremble—no, four it cannot endure." And the first thing on the list is "a slave who becomes a king" (v. 22). Joseph is the slave who is about to become almost the king. Can you imagine what kind of leader he would have been if he had gone from being a slave to becoming the prime minister of Egypt without going through the cleansing and healing process he had just experienced? If he had still been filled with bitterness and resentment when he became the powerful prime minister, he would have been a tyrant. He had to be brought low so that God could get his full attention. He walked with him through a forgiving process that cleared away the debris of his past including dealing with the generational patterns of his unhealthy family background.[1]

The Dream Is Fulfilled

The man who was silent through all the horrible things his brothers did to him, through the journey to Egypt, during his time in Potiphar's household and even in prison, now spoke boldly to Pharaoh. Why didn't Joseph inform the traders who he was and who his father was? His father was a rich, well-known man back in Canaan. That may not have helped him in Egypt, but it would have certainly helped him with the Ishmaelite traders. We don't know why he was silent, but as the rabbis suggest, maybe he was protecting his father's and his brothers' reputations by his silence.

But now in front of Pharaoh, Joseph was bold as he first interpreted Pharaoh's dream and then outlined the plan that Pharaoh was to adopt as a result of his dream. Pharaoh apparently knew Joseph, and he was impressed to the point that he gave him power second only to himself. In about nine years, the dream Joseph had as a young man would be fulfilled when his brothers came in to his palace and "bowed before him with their faces to the ground" (Gen. 42:6). He knew who they were, but they didn't recognize him. After all, the last time they had seen him, he was a boy of 17. Now he was a 39-year-old man, and looked every part the Egyptian.

Why did Joseph go through all this trickery with his brothers? Many have suggested he was getting revenge for what his brothers had done to him. But how is that revenge? If he had wanted revenge, he could have gotten "sweet" revenge. After all, who would question what he was doing with a bunch of Hebrews? Joseph only answered to Pharaoh, and some sheepherders from Canaan wouldn't have bothered him. He could have thrown them in prison, told the servants who were with them who he was, and said, "Take me to my father!" But he didn't.

I think what Joseph was doing was testing his brothers to see if he could be reconciled to them. He knew their language, but he didn't know their hearts. He was very patient. First he questioned them about being spies. In the rabbinical stories, the brothers were afraid of the Egyptians, so they split up and each came into the city through a different gate. And of course, Joseph knew what they had done. When he finished his questioning, he put them all in jail for three days, and when he released them, he required that one of the brothers stay behind. When the rest of the brothers returned for more food, the younger brother must be brought back with them—to prove they weren't spies.

The brothers went home minus Simeon, and of course old Jacob refused to let them take his youngest, Benjamin, back with them. So they just went on with life until they ran out of food again. After much arguing with Jacob, Benjamin was allowed to go with them to Egypt, and once again, Joseph was deceptive with them. But look at what he probably was thinking: "Should I trust them? Have they really changed? Has God worked in their lives?" As he wrestled with questions like these, he still wasn't sure, so he set it up that Benjamin would be forced to stay with him. But Judah, who was also a transitional person in the generational patterns, offered to stay in his place—like a substitutionary sacrifice—and Joseph finally felt safe enough to reveal to all the brothers who he was.

Now we come to one of the two places where God's activity is acknowledged in all we have read about Joseph in the Genesis account. Joseph revealed to them who he was, and then he made it very clear that in spite of what they had done, it was God's hand and purpose that was ultimately at work (see Gen. 45:4-8). Next, there was to be the revealing to Jacob that Joseph was alive and well in Egypt, and then the big reunion as the family moved to Egypt and was together once again.

What about the brothers? Had they been changed after 22 years of guilt? After watching their father grieve over Joseph and after living with the cancer of the soul that comes from holding such a secret, what kind of men had they become? Think of their return home from Egypt as they find their money in the bags of grain. Imagine what went through their minds as they reflected on the accusation that they were spies and spent three days in prison. And now this! How were they going to explain all of this to their father, especially the requirement that Benjamin must return with them the next time? Then think of what must have gone through their minds as on the next journey home, when they had actually talked their father into letting them take Benjamin with them, the prime minister's cup is found in Benjamin's bag and they all head back to Egypt. They weren't just wrestling with guilt feelings—they were genuinely guilty, and God was using all of these things to get their attention.

So What Can We Learn?

The account of Joseph's life is a perfect example of the true meaning of Romans 8:28. Most of the translations of that passage can leave us with a misperception that somehow even bad things become good when you are a believer. But the phrasing of the verse at the beginning of the chapter gives us a deeper understanding, both of the verse and also of the point of Joseph's life. It's clear that bad things happen to all of us. The rain falls on the just and the unjust—equally. But it is God who is at work in all things, seeking to turn the bad into a good that fits in with His purposes for us. And often God's work is hidden from us until some later time. But Joseph sums it all up when he tells his brothers, "You intended to harm me, but God intended it all for good" (Gen. 50:20). Joseph doesn't need revenge, for he now sees the pattern God had for his life. All he needed to do was live for the promise, and even the bad things would somehow fit into the pattern God had for his life. He was able to connect the dots.

God has His purposes for each of our lives. When bad things happen to us, rather than give in and feel like we are a victim of circumstances, we need to remember that God has His purpose for us in all things, and that if we let Him, He will take the bad and somehow make it work for the good in us. For 13 years, nothing went right in Joseph's life. In spite of everything he did to take the lemons he was given and make lemonade, it was still unfair and unjust. He was still a victim! He had every right to simply give up. But he didn't give up. He made the best of everything from a human standpoint, even though he had no clue that anything would ever be different.

We can see his struggle in the names of his children. He named his first child Manasseh, which meant, "God has made me forget all my troubles and everyone in my father's family" (Gen. 41:51). Some might say we are just to forget the past, but an unresolved past that we are trying to forget usually keeps acting itself out in our present. But there was a second child, and his name was Ephraim, which meant "God has made me fruitful in the land of my grief" (v. 52). "Grief" can also be translated as "affliction," "suffering," and even "depression." In any of these places, God made Joseph fruitful, and he can make us fruitful in those places in our lives.

How did Joseph get to the place of fruitfulness in the midst of affliction? How did he move from holey to wholly, and ultimately to holy? It's not a very popular formula. What we see in Joseph's life is a long obedience to God regardless of his circumstances and emotions. In one of the rabbinical stories, Potiphar's wife, Zuleika, is threatening Joseph. She tells Joseph that if he doesn't sleep with her:

"You shall be cruelly oppressed!"

"God helps the oppressed," Joseph answered.

"I shall starve you!"

"God feeds the hungry."

"I shall cast you into prison!"

"God releases the captive."

"I shall force you into the dust!"

"God raises those who are bowed down."

"I shall put out your eyes!"

"God gives sight to the blind."[2]

Somehow, Joseph and God had built together a strong relationship that transcended the circumstances of his life. His walk of faith was consistent as he persevered over time and was found faithful. Walter Brueggemann notes that all too often the "purposes of God are at work in hidden and unnoticed ways."[3] In the account of Joseph, there were no sudden actions or intrusions by God to bring about His purposes. There was no angel to wrestle with, no direct test of faith. It was simply the fact that in everything that went on in Joseph's life, the mysterious and hidden ways of God were at work. Our pastor, Richard Kannwischer, noted this past week that it is never the change that we want that changes everything. It's always the unexpected, and that is certainly the point in Joseph's life.

The other part of the process was the suffering. Joseph did not have an easy life, even when he lived at home. And as we've noted, from the time his brothers almost murdered him, it was downhill for 13 years—one injustice after another! But Joseph was not only holding on to a dream, he was holding on to his heavenly Father. He lived out the truth of Romans 8:28: "God causes everything to work together for the good of those who love God and are called according to his purpose for them." He had to know that at some point, everything would make some sense. He certainly felt the painfulness of all that happened along the way, but he never allowed the pain to take his eyes off the heavenly father, for "the Lord was with Joseph," even as He is with each of us. Joseph was finally able to connect all the dots and to identify God's hand in it all.

6

The Argumentative Saint

The LORD . . . said to Eliphaz the Temanite: "I am angry
with you and your two friends, for you have not spoken accurately
about me, as my servant Job has."

JOB 42:7

I remember when I was a college pastor, I had this idea that college
students needed their pastor to be something of a cynic, feeling
that a bit of questioning was always good when it came to faith. I
also think I had a natural propensity at that time to think that
way. If there was an item of faith that couldn't be proven, I took
the position that said, *I'll believe it when you can prove it to me. Until*
then, I withhold judgment. After all, I was the pastor who was supposed to build up the college group, and that's the way college students supposedly thought.

I'm not sure when it happened, but I remember thinking to
myself that this position of doubting until it was proven true was
not a very solid foundation on which to build my own faith. Too
many things were in the category where judgment was suspended.
It also was not a solid position to help build the faith of those in

the college group. So I made a decision. I decided right then and there that when something couldn't be proven, and when it was a matter of faith, I was going to be a believer, not a "doubter." I wasn't going to be on the fence. Rather than suspend judgment, I started to say to myself, *I'll believe it until it's proven wrong!* And what a difference that made in my relationship with God!

I soon found that taking that position was the right choice; but when it came to bad things happening in my life, that meant I had to believe that in God's eyes, trials and tribulations were good things, not a bad thing. After all, didn't James say, "when troubles come your way, consider it an opportunity for great joy" (Jas. 1:2)? I had to believe what God said through James. My choice took away my option to doubt.

Have you ever asked the question, "Why me?" It's almost an automatic response when bad things happen in our lives. I remember an old Broom-Hilda cartoon in the newspaper. In the first box, there was a black cloud above her with the word "depressed" in the black cloud. In the next box, now the black cloud contained the question, "Why me?" and in the last box, an answer came from outside the box, obviously from God, which answered, "Why not?" Not a very satisfying answer!

Job certainly asked that "Why me?" question. Much of his argument with God and his comforters is an expansion of that question. When we think of Job, we think of suffering, for Job is the ultimate picture of a man who is suffering and in great pain. He not only lost all of his wealth and all of his children, but then he lost his health as well. All he had left was his wife. There is nothing more that could go wrong. We often look at the life of Job as a treatise on suffering, but there is little in the story of Job that provides the answer to the question, "Why me?" or to put it in a more philosophical form, "Why do good people suffer?" The reader of the book of Job is given a partial answer only because we are privy to the conversation between God and Satan regarding Job. There we learn that Job's suffering is a part of what we call "spiritual warfare"—Job is caught in a contest between God and Satan.

I've never liked that answer. I also used to think, *I'll just be a moderate believer because I don't want God and Satan to have any conversations about me.* I thought that if I could blend into the woodwork, Satan would overlook me. And certainly, God wouldn't point me out! Eventually, I saw the ridiculousness of that pattern of reasoning.

Then, also, not all suffering is spiritually based. Sometimes we suffer because of bad decisions we've made, or bad decisions others in our life have made. We'll see in David's life that some of his suffering was a consequence of his adultery with Bathsheba and his murder of her husband, Uriah. And who hasn't had the experience of dreading the consequence of something we've done that was foolish, or even unintentional? But for Job, he was caught in a conflict between God and Satan that he did nothing to cause.

Job is presented as a righteous man. In fact, when God points him out to Satan, he says, "Have you noticed my servant Job? He is the finest man in all the earth. He is blameless—a man of complete integrity. He fears God and stays away from evil" (Job 1:8). But one of the things we also learn about Job early in the story is that he is really almost too righteous, if that is possible. He is certainly overly scrupulous, for after the family got together for several days of celebration, Job would "get up early in the morning and offer a burnt offering for each of them. For Job said to himself, 'Perhaps my children have sinned and have cursed God in their hearts.' This was Job's regular practice" (Job 1:5).

One could say that Job was a perfectionist and a worrier. He thought to himself, *What if one of my children would curse God in their heart and not even know it?* Since it would be better to be safe than sorry, he regularly offered a burnt offering for each of his children. His worrying set him up in a way, for later he says, "What I always feared has happened to me. What I dreaded has come true" (Job 3:25).

What We Don't Know

We don't know who Job really was, nor do we know who wrote the book of Job. Tradition suggests that it was Moses, but there is no evidence to back that up other than tradition. We do know that

the setting of the account takes place during the patriarchal period of Abraham, Isaac, and Jacob. But we don't even know for certain where the village of Uz was located.

One tradition of the Jewish rabbis suggests that Job lived during the time of Jacob, and he was the grandson of Esau. In the commentaries written by these rabbis on Job, they believe that Job's
wife died of exhaustion from taking care of Job while they were
destitute and he was covered with leprosy. His future children
came from a marriage to Dinah, the daughter of Jacob, making
him the son-in-law to Jacob.

Job is described by the rabbinical traditions as "the most pious
Gentile that ever lived, one of the few to hear the title of honor,
'the servant of God' . . . He was entirely worthy of being a member
of the Patriarch's family, for he was perfectly upright, one that
feared God and eschewed evil."[1] Jewish tradition also portrays Job
as being extremely generous with his wealth. He cared for the poor
and the widows, providing food and support without end.

There is another Jewish rabbinical tradition that says Job was
one of the three advisors to Pharaoh in Egypt.[2] When Pharaoh had
his dream about some Hebrew liberating the Israelites, he had
three advisors. One was Balaam, son of Beor; the second was Job,
the man of Uz; and the third was Jethro, the Midianite. Balaam
wanted every male child born to an Israelite woman to be drowned;
Jethro wanted Pharaoh to let the Hebrews alone. When Job was
asked his opinion, for some unknown reason, he was silent. Perhaps he was fearful of being the tiebreaker. As a result, Balaam's argument won the day, and the order was given to drown all the male
babies born to the Hebrews. Having been overruled, Jethro fled to
the land of Midian.

Three years later, when Moses was three and had been rescued
from the Nile River and was adopted by Pharaoh's daughter, he
was sitting on Pharaoh's lap. He grabbed Pharaoh's crown and
placed it on his own head. Balaam remembers the dream, and
urged Pharaoh to order him to be drowned immediately. Bithiah,
Pharaoh's daughter, made a suggestion that the child didn't really
know what he was doing. Again, Job is silent. The rabbis who hold

to this tradition suggest that Job's suffering was a consequence of his silence in Pharaoh's court those two times.

These are some of the attempts of the rabbis to understand why Job suffered, but in reality, the text doesn't give any reason other than that he was caught in the conversation between God and Satan. And when God finally responded to Job's questioning at the end of the book, God again does not answer the question of "why."

In much of the book Job is interacting with his three so-called comforters. These friends accomplished two important things with Job. First, they sat with him in silence for seven days. Jewish tradition says that when someone is in mourning you sit with him or her in silence, and wait for that person to speak first. Perhaps this tradition was already in place when the three comforters sat silently until Job spoke. Regardless of why they were silent, their silence was comforting. The worst thing we can do in our suffering is to isolate ourselves from others. Job wasn't isolated.

The second thing these three comforters did was to cause Job to get angry. If we isolate ourselves from others, it is all too easy to get lost in the despair that Job expresses several times but most clearly all through chapter 3. And if I get lost in my despair I am depressed! My anger turns inward. But if I am legitimately angry with someone else I'm not going to be depressed. Look at what Job says in chapter 3, as he is sinking into despair. He begins with, "Let the day of my birth be erased, and the night I was conceived" (v. 3). He repeats this refrain and then asks, "Why wasn't I born dead? Why didn't I die as I came from the womb?" (v. 11). He finishes with "I have no peace, no quietness. I have no rest; only trouble comes" (v. 26). He is beginning to turn his anger inward upon himself. But his comforters will release him eventually from this temptation.

Arguing with God

Several years ago I was talking with a messianic rabbi. He said to me, "I don't know what's wrong with you Gentiles. You're so thin-skinned. Why can't you just argue something with someone and then let it go?" He went on to say that when Jews argue over something in the Scriptures, for example, they typically get very emotional. But when the argument is finished, they go off arm-in-arm to have coffee together. He then likened that to the Gentile way of arguing, and said, "But for you the argument is never over and all you do when you finish talking is go off and start a new denomination, and you never speak to each other again." I have a lithograph by Charles Bragg called "Midrash," which shows five rabbis arguing as one points to the Scriptures. A Midrash is a commentary on the Scriptures, so Bragg's meaning is that these five rabbis are arguing over the meaning of a text. Every time I look at the picture I think of that conversation with the messianic rabbi, and how, when they closed the book, they went and had coffee together.

In the Old Testament, people argued with God. We already noted this when we looked at Abraham and his intercession with God over the cities of Sodom and Gomorrah. We'll see that Moses argues with God, as does Elijah and Jeremiah. In the Jewish tradition it is called "the law-court pattern of prayer. . . . The book of Job, both in content and structure, represents the climax of the Bible's use and development of the arguing with God motif."[3] Job's arguments are expressed with great intensity as he struggles with God over the suffering of the innocent. What he is really doing is challenging God's justice.

In the midst of Job's challenges to God, he encounters two types of wisdom that seek to answer the question of why the innocent suffer. The first is secular wisdom, which has no answer to the question. It is expressed in Job's wife's statement to him, "Are you still trying to maintain your integrity? Curse God and die" (Job 2:9). Job rejects her statement, and the writer adds the words, "So in all this, Job said nothing wrong" (v. 10).

The second type of wisdom Job encounters is religious wisdom. This is often what people say when they don't know what else to say. Eliphaz starts out with some direct "help." He says:

In the past you have encouraged many people; you have strengthened those who were weak. Your words have sup- ported those who were falling; you encouraged those with shaky knees. But now when trouble strikes, you lose heart. You are terrified when it touches you. Doesn't your reverence for God give you confidence? Doesn't your life of integrity give you hope? (Job 4:3-6).

Not much empathy there. His "counsel" covers two chapters (chapters 4 and 5), and he suggests that Job turn to God to find out what he has done to bring this onto himself. Job responds to Eliphaz in an argument that is directed at God. As he does, he rejects the counsel of his friend. Then in Job 8, Bildad, the second friend, jumps in, only a little more direct with his religious wisdom. He says:

How long will you go on like this? You sound like a blistering wind. Does God twist justice? Does the Almighty twist what is right? Your children must have sinned against him, so their punishment is well deserved. But if you pray to God and seek the favor of the Almighty, and if you are pure and live with integrity, he will surely rise up and restore your happy home. And though you started with little, you will end up with much (Job 8:2-7).

Now we begin to see more clearly what they are trying to say to Job. "Job, your children must have sinned. And if you were honest, you must have sinned as well." The "religious" answer to suffering is that someone must have sinned. It is the same kind of thinking that the disciples articulate in John 9:2 when they ask Jesus, "Why was this man born blind? Was it because of his sins or his parents' sins?" Everything boils down to "someone must have sinned, or else this wouldn't have happened." Job refuses to accept the logic of his friends and continues his defense. He directs his plea to God, and even uses the picture of taking God to court (see Job 9:3). He says:

I will say to God, "Don't simply condemn me—tell me the charge you are bringing against me. What do you gain by oppressing me? Why do you reject me, the work of your

own hands. . . . Again and again you witness against me"
(Job 10:2-3,17).

We see the courtroom terminology all through Job's defense,
but now the third comforter jumps in and hits Job even harder
than the others. Zophar says:

> Shouldn't someone answer this torrent of words? Is a
> person proved innocent just by a lot of talking? Should
> I remain silent while you babble on? When you mock
> God, shouldn't someone make you ashamed? You claim,
> "My beliefs are pure," and "I am clean in the sight of
> God." If only God would speak; if only he would tell you
> what he thinks! If only he would tell you the secrets of
> wisdom, for true wisdom is not a simple matter. Listen!
> God is doubtless punishing you far less than you de-
> served! (Job 11:2-6).

Job answers:

> You people really know everything, don't you? And when
> you die, wisdom will die with you! Well, I know a few
> things myself—and you're no better than I am. . . . As for
> me, I would speak directly to the Almighty. I want to ar-
> gue my case with God himself. As for you, you smear me
> with lies. As physicians, you are worthless quacks. If only
> you could be silent! That's the wisest thing you could do
> (Job 12:2-3; 13:3-5).

After all three have tried to "help" Job, all to no avail, since Job
is really arguing with God, the three comforters begin round two
of their so-called comforting. Eliphaz calls Job a windbag and asks
if he has no fear of God (see Job 15). Bildad wants Job to shut up
(see Job 18), and Zophar is greatly disturbed by Job's insults (see
Job 20). In the middle of this round, Job calls them "miserable
comforters" and adds, "I could say the same things if you were in

my place. . . . My complaint is with God, not with people. I have good reason to be so impatient" (Job 16:4; 21:4).

Then Job continues asking the questions that everyone wants to ask when he or she is suffering. But all it does with his comforters is set off another round of religious wisdom (see Job 22–25), which is even more heartless. This leads to Job's final speech:

> I vow by the living God, who has taken away my rights, by the Almighty who has embittered my soul—as long as I live, while I have breath from God, my lips will speak no evil, and my tongue will speak no lies. I will never concede that you are right, I will defend my integrity until I die. I will maintain my innocence without wavering. My conscience is clear for as long as I live (Job 27:2-6).

His final defense continues for five chapters, where he finally goes through a list of sins and claims his innocence. Job is raising the stakes in his arguments as a challenge to God to intervene. Job follows the Jewish pattern of the law-court pattern of prayer. In it, he first addressed God the judge. Second, he presented the facts of the case. He listed his complaints against God to God. Third, he made a concluding petition or request of God. But before we could get to the fourth element, where there is a divine response to the case, Elihu, a fourth friend, suddenly appears and is angry at both Job for not admitting his sin, and at the three friends for trying to make Job wrong.

Because the other three friends have decided to quit talking, Elihu feels it is time for him to present his thoughts. His case against Job is somewhat more balanced as he speaks for five chapters. His approach is quite different. He argues about the greatness of God, of His power, and of His rightness in all that He does. He also sees repentance differently. The three friends have been trying to get Job to identify and renounce his specific sins. Elihu says that real repentance is a renunciation of our moral authority, which belongs only to God. He feels that Job has been arrogant in challenging God's authority and righteousness. He is preparing the way for God to enter the picture as he accuses Job of not having a big enough God.

God finally interrupts Elihu and begins to challenge Job with unanswerable questions. He first asks, "Who is this that questions my wisdom with such ignorant words? Brace yourself like a man, because I have some questions for you, and you must answer them" (Job 38:2-3). Then God asks Job things such as, "Where does light come from" (Job 38:19), and "can you make lightning appear?" (v. 35), and "are you as strong as God? Can you thunder with a voice like his?" (Job 40:9).

The courtroom motif is finished. Job, at one point in the middle of God's questions, says, "I will cover my mouth with my hand. I have said too much already. I have nothing more to say" (Job 40:4-5). But Job is faced with two more chapters of unanswerable questions before God stops and Job says:

> You asked, "Who is this that questions my wisdom with such ignorance? It is I—and I was talking about things I knew nothing about, things far too wonderful for me. You said, "Listen and I will speak! I have some questions for you, and you must answer them." I had only heard about you before, but now I have seen you with my own eyes. I take back everything I said, and I sit in dust and ashes to show my repentance (Job 42:3-6).

Notice, there is no answer to Job's questions, but it appears that Job is satisfied. I remember hearing that when Catherine Marshall, wife of minister and former chaplain of the U.S. Senate, Peter Marshall, was holding her dying grandchild in her arms, she said, "I would rather have God's presence in my life than any answer to the question 'Why?'" Obviously, Job has now experienced God in a whole new way. It was as if God simply "blew Job's mind" about His greatness and His majesty.

So What Can We Learn?

Why then did Job repent? James 5:11 honors Job for his patience, so that can't be the problem. The only thing I can understand is that

Job repented of having a too limited understanding of God—Job's God was too small. When he was overwhelmed by God's power and majesty, he realized that God was far beyond anything he could possibly imagine. The text makes it very clear that nothing Job said was wrong, so he didn't need to repent over anything he said.

It is interesting that God never rebuked Job for his arguing with Him. Instead, after God finished speaking with Job, He turned to Eliphaz and said, "I am angry with you and your two friends, for you have not spoken accurately about me, as my servant Job has" (Job 42:7). Then God instructed them to make a sin offering and to have Job pray for them. He adds, "My servant Job will pray for you, and I will accept his prayer on your behalf. I will not treat you as you deserve, for you have not spoken accurately about me, as my servant Job has" (v. 8).

Some have wondered why the fourth comforter escaped God's judgment. If you read the six chapters of his speech, you can see the difference. First, he rebuked Job for refusing to admit that he had sinned. But he went on and was angry with the three other comforters, "For they made God appear to be wrong by their inability to answer Job's arguments" (Job 32:3). But when he continued, he didn't attack Job as the other three did. Instead he began to lay the groundwork for what God would say when, beginning in Job 38, He begins to ask Job questions he cannot answer. Elihu did rebuke Job for having too small a view of God, and then proceeded to "present profound arguments for the righteousness of my Creator" (Job 36:3).

What was wrong with the religious wisdom of Job's three friends? It's what's always wrong with religious wisdom. For one thing, it is overly simplistic. It was easy for them to say "You suffer because you've sinned," and presto, the problem should be solved. "Job, it's simple. Confess what you've done wrong and it will all be fixed." Or sometimes, religious wisdom says, "Just trust God more and everything will work out." And we've all experienced the frustration of someone offering us religious wisdom when we are in the middle of hurt and pain and suffering. It doesn't help us, but apparently it helps the one offering the religious wisdom.

A second problem with religious wisdom is that it only deals with the obvious. Why didn't God simply come to Job and say, "Let me tell you, Job, what has been going on." And then God would relate to him what we know from reading the first chapter of Job—that God was allowing Satan to test Job's faithfulness. If the book had ended that way, we might have one more interpretation about suffering, but it didn't end that way. God ended it with the message that when we are struggling, we need a bigger picture of our God.

According to Jewish tradition, we have the right to argue with God. We don't just see this in Abraham and Job, we see it in many of the Psalms. We see Jeremiah doing this in chapter 12, where he asks, "Why are the wicked so prosperous? Why are evil people so happy?" (v. 1). We also see it in Lamentations 3, where the prophet is broken by the fall of Jerusalem, and argues with God in much the same way Job did. We also need to see that it is a healthy part of our relationship with God. And the writer of Hebrews encourages us to "come boldly to the throne of our gracious God. There we will receive his mercy, and we will find grace to help us when we need it most" (Heb. 4:16).

In research on marriage relationships, it has been found that when couples never argue, one or both of them are not invested emotionally in the relationship. In the same way, perhaps the Jewish rabbis were onto something. If we are not able to argue with God, then perhaps we are not that emotionally invested in our relationship with Him. A real, healthy relationship means that we don't always see eye-to-eye, and when we don't, we say something. Job, along with some of the other people of the Old Testament, teaches us that it is good to be able to argue with the Almighty.

The Reluctant Saint

Who am I to appear before Pharaoh?
Who am I to lead the people of Israel out of Egypt?
EXODUS 3:11

Near the beginning of C. S. Lewis's Narnia tales, there is a conversation between the two girls and Mr. and Mrs. Beaver. They are asking about Aslan, the King of the whole wood. Susan asked:

"But shall we see him?

"Why Daughter of Eve, that's what I brought you here for. I'm to lead you where you shall meet him," said Mr. Beaver.

"Is—is he a man?" asked Lucy.

"Aslan a man!" said Mr. Beaver sternly, "Certainly not. I tell you he is the King of the wood and the son of the great Emperor-beyond-the-sea. Don't you know who is the King of Beasts? Aslan is a lion—the Lion, the great Lion."

"Ooh!" said Susan, "I'd thought he was a man. Is he—quite safe? I shall feel rather nervous about meeting a lion."

"That you will, dearie, and no mistake," said Mrs. Beaver; "If there's anyone who can appear before Aslan without their knees knocking, they're either braver than most or else just silly."

"Then he isn't safe?" said Lucy.

"Safe!" said Mr. Beaver; "don't you hear what Mrs. Beaver tells you? Who said anything about safe? 'Course he isn't safe. But he's good. He's the King, I tell you."[1]

Moses had something in common with Lucy, who didn't know about Aslan, the Lion of Judah. At this point in Moses' life, he knew very little about Jehovah, the great I AM. Moses was to discover throughout his last 40 years of life, that God was anything but safe. At first, Moses' experience of God might not even be called good, for there wasn't anyone around to tell him about God. But along the way, Moses became the "friend of God" (see Exodus 33:11a), and he eventually found out that God was good. Indeed, He was very good.

Back to the beginning. For 350 years, God's chosen people had been in Egypt. The rabbis tell us that gradually, Pharaoh became afraid of the growing size and potential power of the Hebrews. They could align themselves with one of Egypt's enemies, and the Egyptians would be outnumbered. So Pharaoh had a plan. He put the Hebrew people to work. At first he paid them for their work, but gradually Pharaoh put harsher and harsher taskmasters over the Hebrews, and then the pay was withdrawn, and eventually they became slaves. As this process unfolded, it must have seemed more and more that the God of Abraham, Isaac, and Jacob had forgotten about His people.

Some of the Hebrew people remained faithful to this God, while most simply forgot about God. After all, God had forgotten about them, so why bother? What good did it do? Among the faithful was a couple from the tribe of Levi, who married, had a son named Aaron and a daughter named Miriam. And then, in the midst of Pharaoh's edict that all Hebrew male babies were to be drowned, a third child was born to this couple—a son. The mother hid him for three months and then gave up trying to hide him. She built a small "ark" and put him in the Nile River, and dispatched Miriam to watch over him.

Now the rabbis have suggested that Pharaoh's daughter was covered with leprosy. When she saw the little "ark" she had one of her attendants bring it to her. She opened it, and when she touched the baby inside, her leprosy was immediately cured. This is not in the biblical account, but maybe that's why she went against her father's command and kept the baby alive. Not only that, but she even unknowingly paid the baby's birth mom to nurse him. And for three years, the baby's mother raised him as a Hebrew, and then he was given to Pharaoh's daughter to raise. She named him Moses. For 37 years, Moses lived in the luxury of Pharaoh's palace as an heir to the throne.

Moses knew he wasn't an Egyptian, and in all likelihood, those three years with his birth mother had imprinted on him some of his Jewish heritage. Tradition says that he not only went out to visit the Hebrews, but he also worked alongside of them. Then, at the age of 40 (see Acts 7:23), Moses decided to do something about what was happening to his people. He saw an Egyptian taskmaster beating a Hebrew man and decided enough was enough. He stepped in and killed the Egyptian and hid his body in the sand. The next day, when he tried to intervene in an argument between two other Hebrew men, they wanted nothing to do with him. They asked him, "Who appointed you to be our prince and judge? Are you going to kill me as you killed that Egyptian yesterday?" (Exod. 2:14). Moses tried to set things right his way and failed miserably; for not only did his fellow Hebrews reject him, but also Pharaoh found out what had happened and tried to kill him. Moses had to flee to the desert.

It appears that for 40 years, Moses was restless. He was like a homeless man. He wasn't an Egyptian and he wasn't really a Hebrew. He was rootless. We see this evidenced when his first son was born and he named him Gershon, which means literally, "stranger there." In that name, Moses was describing the first 40 years of his life.

Restless by the circumstances, Moses hooked up with Jethro, the priest of Midian. Jethro had seven daughters, and eventually Moses married one of them named Zipporah. For 40 more years, Moses was a simple man working as a shepherd for his father-in-law. Think of it. For 80 of his 120 years, Moses was "on the shelf of life." He had tried it his way and failed. So he gave up and accepted the simple life—living in the desert of Midian.

At this point, he had ended up with no faith in God that we can see. He had no knowledge of God, and he certainly had no experience of God. It would be like one of us "wasting" the first two-thirds (about 50 years) of our life and not seeing any hope that the future was going to be any different. Here was a man who had all the advantages of being Pharaoh's grandson—all the learning, skills and languages, the greatest teachers—and then because he felt rootless, he ended up being a nobody. Most people in that position end up depressed and feel hopeless. No wonder he was the reluctant saint who argued with God in the midst of a miracle!

What We Know

Moses could be called a "late bloomer." Most of what we know about him begins when he is 80 years old. During the second 40 years, we see how comfortable Moses was arguing with God, as were Abraham and Job. And like in the story of Abraham, his faith and his walk with God were challenged time and time again. But we will also see how over time his faith grew stronger as his relationship with God became more intimate.

Picture the reluctant saint. He was stopped by a bush that burned but was not consumed. Then the voice of God spoke to him from the bush and told him, "Do not come any closer. . . . Take off your sandals, for you are standing on holy ground" (Exod. 3:5). He was standing in the midst of a miracle, yet he argued in its presence. God spoke directly to Moses and told him, "You must lead my people Israel out of Egypt" (Exod. 3:10). Moses was talking directly with God, yet he said, "Who am I to appear before Pharaoh? Who am I to lead the people of Israel out of Egypt?" (Exod.

3:11). That's more than reluctance—that's telling God He had it all wrong— Moses was saying he was not the man God wanted.

God reassured Moses that He would go with him, but Moses said, "If I go to the people of Israel and tell them, 'The God of your ancestors has sent me to you,' they will ask me, 'What is his name?' Then what shall I tell them?" (Exod. 3:13). And it was here that God began to reveal Himself to Moses in a most intimate way.

When you look back at Moses' life, you can understand his reluctance. He had created a comfortable life in the desert as a shepherd. He probably didn't want anything to do with Egypt or with Pharaoh. But God pressed Moses as He revealed to Moses His name. No one before Moses knew the name of God. In Middle Eastern culture, to know someone's name was to have some kind of power over them. God, in giving Moses His name, was giving him power in his relationship with the I AM—with Jehovah—with Yahweh! Then God said, "This is my eternal name, my name to remember for all generations" (Exod. 3:15).

But Moses was still reluctant. He said, "What if they won't believe me or listen to me? What if they say, 'The Lord never appeared to you?' " (Exod. 4:1). God gave Moses three miraculous things to do in front of the Israelites. First, God told him to throw his staff on the ground, and it turned into a snake. When he picked it up by the tail, it became his shepherd's staff again. Second, he was told to put his hand in his cloak, and when he took it out, it was white with leprosy. When he put it back in his cloak and took it out again, it was healthy again. And third, he was to take water from the Nile River and pour it on dry ground, and it would turn to blood. Surely, all those things should have satisfied Moses' reluctance, but now Moses came up with another excuse—he referred to his speech problem.

Tradition suggests that Moses stuttered, but all the text says is that he gets "tongue-tied" and that his words "get tangled" (Exod. 4:10). It's interesting to note that at the end of Moses' life, this tongue-tied man delivered a three-hour sermon, so his speech problem was eventually resolved. (His final speech makes up most of the book of Deuteronomy.) But for now, Moses was finally out of arguments, and so he just begged off, saying, "Lord, please! Send someone else" (Exod. 4:13). God, in his anger, agreed to have Aaron be Moses' spokesperson.

So Moses headed back to Egypt to meet up with his brother, Aaron. He told Aaron everything God had said to him and showed him the miracles he was to perform for the elders of Israel. And Aaron was on board—no reluctance on his part. Once Moses was back in Egypt, he went before the leaders of Israel, and Aaron spoke the words God gave to Moses. When Moses showed them the signs God gave him, along with the name of God to convince the Israelites that truly he was sent by God, they bowed down and worshipped the Lord. And then Moses went to Pharaoh.

We know what happened, but we may have missed the fact after Moses' and Aaron's first failure to convince Pharaoh. The Hebrew people, even though they had earlier bowed down in acceptance, now turned against them. In fact, they became very angry with Moses and Aaron, for Pharaoh made their work even harder, if not impossible. And once again, Moses turned and argued with God. He said, "Why have you brought all this trouble on your own people, Lord? Why did you send me? Ever since I came to Pharaoh as your spokesman, he has been even more brutal to your people. And you have done nothing to rescue them!" (Exod. 5:22-23). Once again, God patiently reminded Moses that God's plan was bigger than the Israelites, and that He had made a covenant with Abraham to give them the Promised Land. God would deal with Pharaoh on His own timetable. To Moses' credit, he stayed the course.

What We Often Overlook

In his first encounter with God, Moses didn't seem to be impressed. Unlike Lucy, who was afraid to meet Aslan, the Lion of Judah, Moses, in his interaction with God, acted like he was talking to his father-in-law. Perhaps this nonchalant response to God led to a passage that preachers never preach on and teachers never teach. Commentaries have little to say about this short passage, and even the rabbis over the centuries haven't known what to make of it. When Moses got permission from Jethro to leave Midian and go to Egypt, he took his wife and his sons with him. Next we read that, "On the way to Egypt, at a place where Moses and his family had stopped for the night, the LORD confronted him and was about to kill him" (Exod. 4:24).

For years, I had never noticed that short little episode. The whole thing is covered in three verses (see Exodus 4:24-26). When you read it, it seems jarring and out of place. Why would God go through all that conversation to get Moses to do the job, and then seek to kill him? It doesn't make sense. But it's right there in the text. What do we do with the idea that God intended to kill the man He had chosen to be the leader, Moses? In one of the classic Jewish books that recounts the life of Moses, based on the rabbinical stories, this episode is completely ignored.[1] No mention is made of it. Jonathan Kirsch, in his biography of Moses, which is also based on the rabbinical stories, does include it, but there are few stories of the rabbis he can refer to which are related to this event. Kirsch says, "After centuries of silence . . . God decided Moses was the man for the job of liberating the Israelites . . . and he expended a good deal of time, effort and breath in persuading the reluctant Moses to do what was asked of him."[2] Then, when Moses agreed to go, God decided to kill him.

One contemporary rabbi suggests that Moses began to doubt God's plan when he heard that the firstborn in all of Egypt would be killed. This created a "crisis of faith" in Moses. "How can the God who proposed to harden the pharaoh's heart and kill the firstborn of Egypt be the same God who loved Abraham, Isaac, and Jacob?"[3] In his doubting, he decided not to circumcise his newborn son. He defied the covenant with God! The unsafe God would have no part of this crisis, and Moses came close to death. Only the quick action of his wife, Zipporah, saved his life as she acted quickly and decisively made the decision to circumcise Eliezer.

The best some scholars can do is suggest that God was going to kill either Gershon or Eliezer, Moses' sons, because one of them wasn't circumcised. But the text says God was going to kill Moses. Based on this, was Moses to be punished for not circumcising one of his sons? But that doesn't really add up either. Nothing really makes sense of this event.

Perhaps it had something to do with the chutzpah of the reluctant Moses as he argued against God's plan to use him as the liberator of Israel. God didn't want Moses to think He was a pushover. But that doesn't make much sense either. If the circumcision was the issue, why didn't God just tell Moses to get the job done? We will never really know why, this side of heaven.

An interesting part of this short episode is that a woman, using her intuition, was able to divert the intentions of the omnipotent Lord of the Universe to kill Moses. Zipporah was a convert to Judaism, but like Deborah (see Judg. 4) and Esther, she was a courageous woman who saved her husband's life. One thing is for certain, though, this is obviously one of those places where God proves He is clearly not safe. But He is good!

Most sermons I've heard on Moses portray him as a great lawgiver, liberator and leader. We see him the way Michelangelo portrayed him in his famous sculpture—a powerful man and great leader. Yes, at times he could be strong and heroic, but there were also times when he was timid and "tortured with self-doubt at key moments in his life."[4] The Bible says he "was very humble—more humble than any other person on earth" (Num. 12:3). He could be the mild and meek shepherd, but he could also be the ruthless warrior. In truth, we have no idea what he looked like. Images of Moses reflect his strengths while ignoring his weaknesses. Yet, in spite of that mix of impressions, the Bible makes it clear that "there has never been another prophet in Israel like Moses, whom the LORD knew face to face" (Deut. 34:10). In the Jewish tradition, he is called "Moses, our Master." To the slaves in Colonial America, he was their hero. They sang their spirituals that said things like, "Go down, Moses. Set your people free."

So What Can We Learn?

The story of Moses is really a story about God, in the same way that the Narnia tales are really a story about Aslan, the Lion of Judah. We have already noted that God made himself known to Moses by telling him His name. He is the I AM—Jehovah—Yahweh. The one who is eternally present. In response to Moses' complaint, God said, "I am Yahweh—'the LORD.' I appeared to Abraham, to Isaac, and to Jacob as El-Shaddai—'God Almighty'—but I did not reveal my name, Yahweh, to them" (Exod. 6:2-3). One of the rabbinic stories says that the name Yahweh was known before God's encounter with Moses, but that it had been forgotten by the Israelites during their captivity. But the name had been held secretly by the elders of Israel and passed on to each succeeding generation. That is why later, when Moses came before the elders of Israel and was able to give them the name of God, they believed him.

The name Yahweh is translated in our Bible as "the LORD (with small capital letters). It is called the Tetragrammaton by the Jews, for it is a word spelled in Hebrew with four letters. These four letters correspond in English to YHWH. There is a long and sacred tradition in Judaism regarding this name of God. It is never to be spoken. If someone is reading aloud the text in Hebrew, and they came to the word YHWH, they would substitute the Hebrew word "Adonai." This is actually the Hebrew word for Lord (with lower case after the first capital letter) and literally means, "The Name."

When there was the Tabernacle, and then when the Temple was built, the name of God—YHWH—could only be said by the high priest, and only when he was in the Holy of Holies once each year, on Yom Kippur, the Day of Atonement. After the Temple was destroyed in A.D. 70, there was no place that the name Yahweh was to be uttered.

Scholars over the centuries have tried to understand the Tetragrammaton by looking at the different possible roots of the word. They have suggested that the meaning of the name includes "the Eternal One," "the Destroyer," "The Thunderer," "the One Who Succors," and "the One Who Roars," which sounds like Aslan, the Lion of Judah. When God was talking to Moses, he said that this name had never been given to anyone before Moses, yet the name YHWH appears in Genesis on five occasions. But since we believe that Moses wrote the first five books of the Bible—which comprise the Torah—the notes in the *New Living Translation* Study Bible suggest that "Moses, the author of Genesis, was inspired to insert that name in those places in Genesis where God's grace and his nature as covenant-keeper were apparent."[5] This name gave Moses, and gives us, a powerful insight into the character of God. It is the beginning of Moses' journey in getting to really know who God is.

Later on, after they leave Egypt, and before starting the journey to the Promised Land, God added more information about Himself by showing his "awesome glory" to all the people (see Exodus16:7,10). Here we learn more about the character of Yahweh. God's glory is not some passive or abstract concept, nor is it some glowing thing. In this context, it is really quite different from what we typically think of when we think of glory. In the Jewish mind, glory has always been some heavy or solid concept that visibly expresses something absolute about God. In Exodus 16, it has several concrete expressions. First, God's glory is seen in giving assurance and sustenance for Israel. They are without food, and like people with a very immature faith, the first time adversity comes, they turn on their leader and want to undo all that God had done for them—they wanted to go back to Egypt! But God's glory provides manna for them, the bread of angels, and meat in the form of quail.

God's glory is also seen in the literal presence of Yahweh during the journey of the Israelites. It is seen in the cloud that went before them by day, and the pillar of fire that stood over them at night. Here God's glory is not only for the benefit of Israel but also for all mankind who could see the cloud and the pillar of fire. And His glory goes beyond the nations of the world to include all of creation. The psalmist wrote, "The heavens proclaim the glory of God. The skies display his craftsmanship" (Ps. 19:1).

There are three more things we learn about God in the story of Moses. First, it is clear that God is an interactive God. He can be moved by our prayers. We see this in Abraham's argument with God over Sodom and Gomorrah. Abraham started asking God that if there were at least 50 righteous souls in those two cities, would that keep God from destroying those cities. When God agrees, Abraham drops the number to 40, and finally ends with 10, and God agrees.

In His relationship with Moses, there are a number of occasions when God was so angry at Israel that He was ready to give up on them. Each time, Moses argued with God—remember that it is a form of prayer—and each time, God changed His mind. I think we place so much emphasis on the passage that says, "Jesus Christ is the same yesterday, today, and forever" (Heb. 13:8) that we think God is locked in and there is no reason to pray. It almost becomes fatalistic. But Moses shows us a number of times that God is not locked in and we see that our prayers can change the mind of God.

For example, in Exodus 32, when Israel made the idol—the golden calf—God said to Moses on Mt. Sinai, "Quick! Go down the mountain! Your people whom you brought from the land of Egypt have corrupted themselves. . . . Now leave me alone so my fierce anger can blaze against them, and I will destroy them" (Exod. 32:7,10). Notice the phrase "Your people." God wanted nothing to do with Israel, and it was up to Moses to change His mind. Moses knew how to argue with God now. He pointed out what it would look like in Egypt if God destroyed the people He rescued. "So the Lord changed his mind about the terrible disaster he had threatened to bring on his people" (Exod. 32:14). But even though God changed His mind, there were still consequences for the people who had so grievously sinned.

Again, in Numbers 14, God was fed up with the Israelites. He said to Moses, "How long will these people treat me with contempt? Will they never believe me even after all the miraculous signs I have done among them? I will disown them and destroy them with a plague" (Num. 14:11-12). Once again, Moses argued with God, using the same argument as before. God, how do you think that will look back in Egypt? This time God said, "I will pardon them as you have requested" (v. 20). But again, there were consequences. It's as if God and Moses were becoming like a cranky old married couple, with God getting frustrated and angry, and Moses praying God out of His anger.

The second thing we learn from the relationship between God and Moses is that there were some things on which God would not and could not be moved. On some things, God is good, but He is not safe. We saw this in His attempt to kill Moses. We see it again when two of the sons of Aaron, Nadab and Abihu, who were priests, "put coals of fire in their incense burners and sprinkled incense over them. In this way, they disobeyed the Lord by burning before him the wrong kind of fire, different than he had commanded. So fire blazed forth from the LORD's presence and burned them up, and they died there before the LORD" (Lev. 10:1-2). No negotiation on this one! No arguing with God about this!

Moses said to Aaron, "This is what the LORD meant when he said, 'I will display my holiness through those who come near me. I will display my glory before all the people.' And Aaron was silent" (Lev. 10:3). Aaron's two sons knew better. They were singled out and invited to the feast that celebrated the sealing of the covenant. God summoned Moses and Aaron to the feast, along with 70 of the elders of Israel, and then also invited Aaron's two oldest sons, Nadab and Abihu. These 74 men actually "saw the God of Israel (Exod. 24:10). Yet the two sons became careless in their relationship with God, and were killed.

We see a similar consequence in the rebellion of Korah. Korah was a Levite and was described by the rabbis as Pharaoh's treasurer. He obviously had a plush lifestyle while in Egypt, and struggled with the hardships of the journey through the wilderness. So one day he conspired with two others, Dathan and Abiram, to incite a rebellion against Moses. The rabbis show these three men as being a constant "thorn in the flesh" for Moses, and that they were the ones who informed Pharaoh that Moses had killed the Egyptian. At this point, though, Korah is prepared to act. He recruited 250 of the leaders of Israel to join him. He said to Moses and Aaron, "You have gone too far! The whole community of Israel has been set apart by the LORD, and he is with all of us. What right do you have to act as though you are greater than the rest of the LORD's people?" (Num. 16:3).

Moses "fell face down on the ground" (Num. 16:4) when he heard what they said, and then said that "tomorrow morning the

Lord will show us who belongs to him and who is holy" (v. 5).
When they gathered the next morning, again Moses and Aaron
fell face down to the ground and prayed that God would not deal
with all the people, but only with the leader. Then God said to
Moses, "Tell all the people to get away from the tents of Korah,
Dathan, and Abiram" (v. 24). When Moses finished speaking, the
earth opened up and swallowed not only the three men but also
their whole households and all their followers. And then fire de-
voured all those who were part of the 250 leaders who had joined
Korah and weren't swallowed up by the earth. God is good, but
He is certainly not safe.

Those events introduce the third thing we learn about God.
He has an agenda for all of us, and that agenda is for us to grow in
holiness. When it comes to holiness, there is nothing to negotiate
or argue about! Beginning in Leviticus 17, and continuing through
Leviticus 26, God spells out for Israel what He means by holiness.
It includes how we worship, sexual morality, personal conduct,
obedience, the celebration of the festivals and concern for the
poor. It may seem to us today that God isn't very serious about
our holiness, for the earth doesn't swallow us, and the fire of the
Lord does not consume us. But the New Testament reminds us
that "you must be holy because I am holy" (1 Pet. 1:16).

Moses is the only man who encountered God face to face and
lived. From that time forward, Moses had to cover his face with a
veil, for the people could not look at him. In Exodus 34, we read
that after Moses had spent 40 days and 40 nights on Mount Sinai
with the Lord, and he descended from the mountain, he "wasn't
aware that his face had become radiant because he had spoken to
the LORD" (v. 29). Aaron and the people were afraid to come near
him, and because of that, Moses wore a veil over his face for the
next 40 years (see vv. 34-35).

We don't know what was so scary about his face, but when this
passage was first translated into Latin, it read in such a way that
suggested that Moses had sprouted horns on his head. That's why
in Michelangelo's great statue of Moses, he has a set of horns on
his head. There's no evidence in the original text to suggest such

a thing, but he was disfigured in such a way that the people were afraid. It says that Moses wore the veil, except when he went into the tent to converse directly with God.

So What Can We Learn?

The account of Moses and the Israelites is rich in lessons that can be applied to our lives. Countless sermons have made that point very effectively. But what can we learn from some of the things we have discussed in this chapter? I think the idea that God is good but He is not safe is the most important lesson. We, like Moses, want to be a friend of God. He invites us to enjoy an intimate relationship with Him. But in that intimacy, we must never lose sight of the fact that He is God and He is holy, and we cannot take that relationship lightly, as Nadab and Abihu did.

It's important also to watch Moses as he confronted the rebellious Korah and his co-conspirators. He first fell to the ground and prostrated himself facedown. He began, not with confronting Korah, but with coming before the Lord in humility. He did this in his first encounter and again, the next morning, when God was to show who was in charge. He didn't mess around and assume that since he was the friend of God, he could act cavalierly in his attitude toward God. He never forgot that no matter how intimate his relationship with God was, he was encountering the majestic, all-powerful Lord of the Universe! We need to have that same attitude.

At the same time, Moses had an ongoing dialogue with the Lord—with Yahweh. All too often our prayer life may be fervent and frequent, but it is a monologue. Just as we saw Moses pleading with God not to destroy the rebellious people of Israel, we also see that in his dialogue with Yahweh, he influenced God's actions. Moses had the kind of relationship with God that we seek as well. When he would meet with God "inside the Tent of Meeting, the LORD would speak to Moses face to face, as one speaks to a friend" (Exod. 33:11). This doesn't mean we will always literally need to hear God's voice in response—that may only happen on a rare occasion. But if we approach our praying in a conversational way, as friend to friend, but with great respect, we may not only be changed, but God may also be influenced.

The rabbinical tradition describes the end of Moses' life in this way: "God kills Moses with a single divine kiss—just as God breathed life into Adam at the moment of Creation, he draws out the last breath of life from Moses with his own lips."[6] That image may not fit our way of thinking, but it is one last picture of the intimacy that Moses shared with Yahweh, the God of All!

The Pampered Saint

*You will become pregnant and give birth to a son, and his hair must
never be cut. For he will be dedicated to God as a Nazirite from birth.
He will begin to rescue Israel from the Philistines.*

JUDGES 13:5

Gary was the pastor of a church. It wasn't a big church, so there
was only a part-time secretary there in the mornings, along with
Gary. As he told me his story, he commented on how difficult it
was to stay focused on his sermon preparation, especially when he
was alone in the church office. For a diversion, he started looking
at pornography. Soon his sermon preparation time started to give
way to his fascination with the pornography. He became addicted,
and like in any addiction, he wanted more and soon found himself
participating in several pornographic chat rooms.

This went on for a while, and then he met Gina in one of the
chat rooms. Gina lived on the East Coast, and Gary lived on the
West Coast, so it seemed safe enough. They talked, and they
talked sex. And soon the chats with Gina took the place of the
pornographic sites. Gina wasn't married, but Gary was. Gina had

some extra money, so eventually she bought him an airline ticket so they could meet. Of course, all during this time, Gary managed to put together a sermon a week and continued to pastor his church.

Gary found a way to "explain" to his wife the purpose of the trip. So now he was into major lies at home. It was set up that Gina and Gary would meet in the middle of the country—that way no one would know either of them. When he and Gina met, it was exciting. Sex was never like this at home. I think it was the third trip Gary took to meet Gina when his wife started to think something was wrong. She checked and found out about the affair. She not only confronted Gary, but she also contacted the denominational leader for their district. That's when they came to me for counseling. I hate to say it, but the counseling for the marriage never had a chance. Gary was hooked on Gina and was resolute in his choice to give up everything he had—his family, his kids, his church and his ministry—all for his new life with Gina. The counseling shifted to helping Gary's wife and kids deal with the pain of what they were experiencing.

Pornography is a vast business. Every second, people are spending over $3,000 on pornography. It is estimated that in the United States, revenue from pornography of all sorts is larger than the National Football League franchises, Major League Baseball franchises, and the National Basketball Association teams combined. Every 39 minutes, a new pornography site is being set up on the Internet.[1] Twelve percent of all websites on the Internet are pornographic—that is 4.2 million sites. When it comes to email, 8 percent of all emails sent are some form of pornography.[2] Exposure to pornography begins, on average, at the age of 11. By the time that child turns 16, 90 percent of his or her peers will have viewed a pornography website.[3] Ten percent of all adults admit to being addicted to pornography, and 37 percent of pastors admit to being addicted.[4] It's big business!

Samson would have liked Gary; they had similar addictions. One might even say that Samson was the first sex addict mentioned in the Bible. Some might say it was Judah who was first.

He is the one who slept with the prostitute, only to find out some time later that it was his daughter-in-law whom he had kept from her rightful husband. But Samson had a more overt problem than Judah. He saw a pretty girl in a Philistine town and demanded that his parents arrange a wedding. When that fell apart, he spent the night with a prostitute in Gaza, and then he allowed himself to be duped in the familiar story of Delilah. Women and anger were his downfall. And the problem of anger in men caught up in sex addiction is well documented.

What We Know

More space is given to the life of Samson in the book of Judges than to any of the other judges, even though he was not much of a judge. One of the first things we encounter in the story of Samson is the familiar situation of a woman who is barren and to whom God has promised a child. Sarah, Rebekah, Rachel, and eventually Hannah, who was to be Samuel's mother, join Manoah's wife in the line-up of barren wives. (The rabbis gave Manoah's wife the name Zelilponit.)

When the angel visited Zelilponit to announce that she would give birth to a son, he also told her that her child would be dedicated to God from birth as a Nazirite. Samuel's mother, Hannah, made a promise to God that if she could bear a son, he would be a Nazirite as well. What is a Nazirite? To understand, we need to go back to Numbers, chapter 6, where Moses instructs the people in what it means to take a Nazirite vow. Moses said, "If any of the people, either men or women, take the special vow of a Nazirite, setting themselves apart to the LORD in a special way, they must give up wine and other alcoholic drinks" (Num. 6:2-3). There were other dietary restrictions, including grapes or anything made from grapes, including wine and vinegar. They were not to cut their hair during the period of their vow, and they were not to have any contact with anything dead. If they in any way broke their vow, either intentionally or by accident, they must shave their head, rededicate themselves and start over again.

The Nazirite vow was taken very seriously in biblical times, and it was a way that a person could express devotion and gratitude to God. Someone who wasn't from the tribe of Levi, and therefore not a priest, could take this vow, which separated the person from the normal way of life to a more priestly way of life. The term "Nazirite" comes from a Hebrew word that means "to separate." So with the vow, the person would separate himself from his normal lifestyle and live more in accord with the lifestyle of a priest. In the case of Samson, and apparently of Samuel, the Nazirite vow was made before their birth and was made by their mothers. It was to be a way of life for each of them.

The other well-known part of the story of Samson is his dalliance with Delilah. Delilah was a Philistine, the enemy of Israel. She was being paid by the Philistines to find out the secret to Samson's strength. Three times she tested him, and each time he lied to her about the source of his strength. She nagged and pestered him until he finally told her the truth. And then she had his head shaved, and Samson was no longer the strong man. He paid a great price for his addiction to Delilah—he not only lost his strength, but he also lost his freedom and both of his eyes. When it came to his addiction, like any addict that is confronted with the consequences of his addiction, Samson was filled with shame and guilt, but it was too late!

What We Often Overlook

God responded to the barrenness of Manoah and his wife with a visitation by an angel. The angel announced to Zelilponit, "Even though you have been unable to have children, you will soon become pregnant and give birth to a son" (Judg. 13:3). The angel goes on to warn her not to eat any forbidden foods, nor to drink any alcoholic beverages, including wine. He then added that the son would be a "Nazirite from birth. He will begin to rescue Israel from the Philistines" (v. 5).

When Zelilponit told her husband, he was concerned that perhaps she hadn't gotten things straight, and so he asked God to have the angel return and give them more instructions. Nothing like getting your early parenting skills directly from the Lord. Again, the angel appeared to Zelilponit, but she ran and got Manoah to come and meet the "man." The instructions were the same—Zelilponit was to live as a Nazirite during her pregnancy, and Samson was to be a Nazirite from birth.

Now think about what Manoah and Zelilponit must have experienced. Here are two old people, who have had no children, suddenly faced with the task of raising a child. And not just any child, but a special child whose birth was announced to them by an angel! Put together the older age of the parents and the special nature of the child and one can imagine what kind of parenting Samson received—or didn't receive. If we thought Joseph was a spoiled brat, Samson was probably even more spoiled, and the rest of the account of his life proves that point.

We see their ineffective parenting skills when Samson announced that he saw a pretty Philistine woman and wanted to marry her. He said, "A young Philistine woman in Timnah caught my eye. I want to marry her. Get her for me" (Judg. 14:2). No discussion, just a demand! When his parents tried to reason with him, his response was "Get her for me! She looks good to me" (v. 3). Samson had a feeling of entitlement—what he wanted he was supposed to get. He was self-absorbed and irresponsible. And he was disrespectful to his parents and to God. The Israelites, including Samson, were commanded by God not to intermarry with the people of the land, especially the Philistines, who were probably at the top of the forbidden list (see Deut. 7:3; Josh. 23:12-13). But that meant nothing to Samson.

On the way to Timnah to arrange the wedding, Samson encountered a lion. He broke its jaw with his bare hands and apparently left it there to die. So on this occasion he was not in the presence of someone or something that had died, which was a part of the Nazirite vow. But as we will see, the vow meant very little to Samson. There is a paradox here, for the vow is in seeming conflict with his calling, which is to "begin to rescue Israel from the Philistines" (Judg. 13:5), which would involve Samson killing Philistines, not marrying one of them.

It must have taken some time to make all the arrangements for the wedding, for when Samson went back down to Timnah for the wedding, the lion was now dead, and a swarm of bees had made some honey in the carcass. He scooped some out and ate it on the way to the wedding. Now this was a direct violation of the Nazirite vow, but it didn't bother Samson, and apparently didn't yet bother God either, for God continued to use Samson.

In his arrogance, Samson came up with an impossible riddle for his Philistine wedding companions. The riddle went like this:

Out of the one who eats came something to eat; out of the strong came something sweet (Judg. 14:14).

If they solved the riddle, Samson would buy them each a fine linen robe and some festive clothing. It they couldn't solve the riddle, then they must each buy him a fine linen robe and a set of festive clothing, adding up to 30 robes and 30 sets of festive clothing.

There were seven days of celebration for the wedding, so they had seven days to solve it. With each passing day, the Philistine men began to panic. They threatened to burn down the bride's father's house if she didn't get from Samson the meaning of the riddle. So she, with tears, accused Samson of hating her. He must prove his love for her by telling her the answer to the riddle. He refused at first, but he had a weakness for women. So, predictably, he gave in and told her the answer.

His bride-to-be immediately betrayed him and told the answer to her kinsmen. They solved the riddle, so Samson had to pay up. He knew how they knew the answer, for he said to them, "If you hadn't plowed with my heifer, you wouldn't have solved my riddle!" (Judg. 14:18). In his anger, he killed 30 Philistine men, took their belongings and gave it to the 30 groomsmen. And then he skipped out on the actual wedding and returned home.

After the passage of some time, Samson's anger calmed down and he decided to take a goat as a gift to his "wife-to-be." But when he got to her father's house, he found out that the father had married off his daughter to the best man. According to ancient Jewish tradition, giving the bride to the best man was forbidden. Obviously, the father had no respect for either tradition or for Samson. This time, Samson became extremely angry. "He went out and caught 300 foxes. He tied their tails together in pairs, and he fastened a torch to each pair of tails. Then he lit the torches and let the foxes run through the grain fields of the Philistines" (Judg. 15:4-5). All of the Philistines' grain was destroyed, as were their vineyards and their olive groves. Must have been sweet revenge for Samson.

Of course, this led to a declaration of war by the Philistines against Israel. When the Israelites asked what this was all about, they said they were looking for Samson. Give them Samson and there would be no war. So 3,000 Israelites went looking for Samson, and finally found him hiding in a cave. He was afraid his own countrymen were going to kill him, and when he found out that wasn't their intention, he allowed them to tie him up and deliver him to the Philistines. When they turned him over to the Philistines, they shouted with joy at their apparent victory, but it was a short-lived victory, for Samson quickly broke the ropes that bound him, and with the jawbone of a donkey, he killed 1,000 Philistines that day.

Why did I refer to Samson as a sex addict? When you read the story of Samson in Judges 13-16, all of his troubles were related to women, and even included a prostitute. After he killed the 1,000 Philistines, he went on with his life. But at the same time, the Philistines were still obsessed with capturing and killing him. He didn't care; after all, he was so strong that he feared nothing. As part of moving on with his life, Samson, in his obsession with sex, went to the Philistine town of Gaza to spend the night with a prostitute.

Obviously, the Philistines were keeping track of every move Samson made. So when he made the arrangements with the prostitute, it was no secret. The men of Gaza knew exactly where he was. So they locked the city gate and set up guards in the guardhouse. Their plan was to kill him when he left Gaza in the morning. With the gates locked, they slept believing Samson would be caught. But Samson got up at midnight, and locked gates were no problem for him. He simply lifted them out of the ground, both gates and posts, and carried them on his shoulders some 40 miles away. This event caused the rabbis to write about Samson as if he were a giant of some sort. In order to carry the locked gate complete with posts on his shoulders, he must have been a giant, for the gate system was probably at least 12 feet across.

The other thing the rabbis said in their brief comments on Samson was that even though he was extremely strong, he also had a weak side. "He allowed sensual pleasure to dominate him. The consequence was that 'he who went astray after his eyes, lost his eyes.' "[5] Even this severe punishment produced no change of heart. He continued his old life of profligacy in prison. The rabbis said the Philistines promoted his sexual appetite, perhaps thinking that maybe one of his progeny would be big and strong like him.

Like anyone struggling with an addiction, Samson believed he was in control. The harsh truth was that he was seriously out of control, and that no matter what he did, he would continue to spin out of control until his very last act when he pulled the Philistine temple down on himself and 3,000 of the Philistine leaders. What he could have been and should have been was tragically lost—a loss of a man who had the tremendous potential to be a great leader for Israel.

Look at Samson's life. He had supernatural blessing and supernatural strength. But because there was no discipline in his life, he coasted along. He must have believed he was invincible. But when his wife-to-be shed tears and begged him for the secret to the riddle, he gave in. After she betrayed him, he still wanted to marry her, only to find out it was too late. Then with Delilah, the scene was repeated. Three times she begged him for the secret to his strength, and each time he toyed with her. And each time, the Philistines tried to use Delilah's information, but each time they failed. The actions of the Philistines didn't even faze Samson—he stayed with Delilah.

Wouldn't you think that after the second time, and certainly after the third time Delilah betrayed him, he would leave? But not Samson! Instead, on the fourth time, he ended up giving Delilah the secret of his strength. Three times she had betrayed him; but in his addiction, he was blinded to it—he was in denial. And with the fourth betrayal, the consequences were huge—not only did he lose his freedom, but he also lost his eyes. And perhaps in his literal blindness, he began to see that the idea that he was in control was an illusion. In truth, he was being controlled by the lust of his eyes—by his addiction to sex, even with the enemy.

So What Can We Learn?

The Bible tells us that "Samson judged Israel for twenty years during the period when the Philistines dominated the land" (Judg. 15:20). He was not a leader, nor did he mobilize the people of Israel against the Philistines. He was simply an irritant to Israel's enemy. His judgeship was self-centered. And because of that, it became an example of what could have been. One wonders how it would have been different if he had taken his Nazirite vow seriously. What would have happened if he had exercised leadership instead of self-indulgence? When he killed the thousand Philistines, what could Israel have done if he had rallied the men into an army and they, with God's help, had thrown off the domination of the Philistines? Instead, Samson didn't lead. He was too obsessed with the Philistine women, and his Nazirite vow was meaningless to him.

Here's the point. God did work through Samson, in spite of himself. In the part of the story about his possible wedding, neither his mother nor his father realized that "the LORD was at work in this, creating an opportunity to work against the Philistines, who ruled over Israel at that time" (Judg. 14:4). Perhaps God recognized the limitations of Samson as a leader but settled for Samson's policy of harassment. Unfortunately, the policy of harassment didn't change the domination of the Philistines over Israel, although it was a constant distraction for them as they tried and failed to contain the threat of Samson.

What do we learn about God in the story of Samson? One thing is clear: God can use whatever we give Him, whether it is big or small. His purposes transcend our distractions. Samson was obsessed with the Philistine women, so God used Samson's sinful ways to accomplish what God wanted to accomplish. But at the same time, there must have been a sadness in God for what could have been accomplished had God had a willing leader. We see this truth in the story of Gideon, one of the earlier judges in Israel. The Israelites were dominated by the Midianites at that time period. And war was declared.

As Israel prepared to go to battle against the Midianites, Gideon raised an army of 32,000 men—not much of an army when the enemy numbered 135,000. And then God told Gideon his army was too big. God told Gideon that any of the men who were timid or afraid should go home. Twenty-two thousand men went home, leaving Gideon with an army of 10,000 men. Again, God said it was too many, so God told Gideon to divide the men by the way they drank water at the river.

In one group Gideon put the men who had cupped the water in their hand to drink, and in the other group he put the men who had got down on their knees to drink. In the group that had cupped the water in their hand, there were only 300 men, and I am sure that as Gideon saw the disparity in the numbers, he was hoping in his heart for the group of 9,700 men. But he probably also knew that God was going to choose the 300. And with 300 dedicated men, and with Gideon's faith and leadership in the short battle that ensued, there were soon more than 120,000 dead Midianites.

If God could do that through the faith and dedication of one judge—Gideon—what could he have done with an obedient and dedicated Samson? In spite of his problems, Samson is still included in the list of faith in Hebrews 11, right alongside Gideon. We'll never know how different Samson's story could have been, that's not the point. But we can learn from both Gideon and Samson, who gave us both sides of the story. One walked in faith; the other walked in self-indulgence and addiction.

What about our own life story? Hopefully, we don't want to settle only for what we can see; we need to look carefully at what that is and ask God to give us a new vision. For Gideon, the vision was faith. May it be so with all of us.

The Jealous Saint

As Samuel grew old, he appointed his sons to be judges over Israel. . . .
But they were not like their father, for they were greedy for money.
They accepted bribes and perverted justice.

1 SAMUEL 8:1,3

Bill Hybels, pastor of the Willow Creek Church, tells the story of something that happened to him in the second grade. His teacher read to the class a story from the Old Testament about a man named Eli and a young boy named Samuel. It was the story of how Samuel kept hearing his name being called. Each time he heard his name, he would run and wake up Eli. When this happened three times, Eli told him to just wait and listen for God. When the story was finished, the kids ran out to recess, but young Billy Hybels stayed behind and asked the teacher, "Does God still speak to little boys?" She assured him that God still speaks.

As Billy turned to run outside to join the other kids at recess, the teacher called him back and reached into the top drawer of her desk and said that she had something for him. She handed him a folded piece of paper and said that there was a poem written on it.

Later that night, he read the poem. He read it not once, but three times, and then he decided to memorize the poem.

The next day, his teacher asked him if he had read the poem, and when he told her he had not only read it, but had memorized it, she was surprised. She asked him if he could recite it for her, and as he said, he "took up the dare." "Oh, give me Samuel's ear," he said, "an open ear, O Lord, alive and quick to hear each whisper of Thy Word; like him to answer to the call, and to obey Thee first of all."[1] Ever since that experience, Hybels' ministry as a pastor has been characterized by his patiently listening for the whispers of God.

The story of Samuel begins as troubled Israel was waiting, but not listening. As a nation, they had hit bottom. The book of Judges ends with the words, "In those days Israel had no king; all the people did whatever seemed right in their own eyes" (Judg. 21:25). Israel was politically weak, dominated by their enemy, the Philistines. As a result, they were economically devastated. They were in moral chaos, with everyone doing whatever they wanted. Life was filled with brutality and violence, and God had disappeared, leaving Israel barren spiritually. Can you imagine what it must have been like to live during this "in-between" time—the period of time between the book of Judges and the book of 1 Samuel? Life was full of fear. Confusion was all around, and no one knew what would come next. At best, it was a time of waiting; but no one knew what he or she was waiting for. At worst, it was a time of despair and emptiness. There is only the hint in that final verse of the book of Judges about what they were waiting for. Whether they knew it or not, they were waiting for a king.

In the midst of the waiting, the story of God's relationship with Israel resumes with the story of a barren, desperate and depressed woman named Hannah. She was waiting for a child in a state of hopelessness. In the case of Hannah, the barrenness would end, and the waiting would lead to her having a son named Samuel. The rabbinical stories don't have much to say about Samuel, but they do tell us a little about Elkanah, Samuel's father, and about Hannah, his mother. According to the rabbis, Elkanah was the only pious man in his generation. He stood alone, like Abraham stood alone. Three times a year, as required, he would head to Shiloh to worship the Lord. And each time he went, he would go a different route so he could encourage all those he met to join him in worshipping the Lord.

He and Hannah had been married for 10 years, with no children. It was Hannah who suggested he marry another wife so that he could have children. He did. He married Peninnah, and she gave him children. But Peninnah was jealous of Hannah's relationship with their husband, and so the rabbis said she would taunt Hannah with questions like, "Did you forget to get up and wash your kids this morning and then send them to school?" Or perhaps she would ask, as they journeyed to Shiloh, "Where are your kids, Hannah, did you lose them?" This went on for years, and "each time, Hannah would be reduced to tears and would not even eat" (1 Sam. 1:7).

In that culture, as with Jacob and Rachel, the way to gain your husband's favor was to have children, especially to have sons. But just as Jacob favored and loved Rachel, Elkanah favored and loved Hannah more than Peninnah. On this particular journey to Shiloh, Elkanah noticed that Hannah was crying, and he said to her something I would think every wife would love to hear her husband say. He said, "Why be downhearted just because you have no children? You have me—isn't that better than having ten sons?" (v. 8). Wow! What a man! But what a letdown it must have been to him when Hannah shook her head and said, "No"!

Since they were at Shiloh, when Hannah couldn't eat, she instead would pray. She prayed so fervently that Eli, the priest, thought she was drunk. As she prayed, she made a bargain with God. She said that if God would give her a son, she would give him back to God as a Nazirite. (Remember Samson? He had also been given to God but failed to keep the vow.) The Nazirite vow meant being consecrated to God and showing it by not cutting his hair, not drinking wine and not being defiled by the presence of a corpse. Hannah wanted a son so much that she was willing to give him back to God. And as we will see, this wasn't some symbolic "giving back." Several years later, when Samuel was weaned,

Hannah literally gave him back to God when she turned him over to Eli, the priest. She left him at Shiloh. She had made a vow and she kept it. So now the barrenness of Hannah was resolved, and Samuel's entrance marked the beginning of Israel's moving out of barrenness.

What We Know

The arrival of Samuel in God's story with the Israelites was the first movement in the next stage of Israel's development as a nation, and a move forward in their relationship with God. When Samuel came on stage, Israel was a scattered bunch of tribal people who weren't really connected to each other. They were rivals and didn't know how to come together, even to defend themselves. But by the time Samuel leaves the stage, Israel was well on her way to becoming a solid nation. Samuel was the human factor empowering those changes. He was the final judge, and as such, he became the moving force in Israel's spiritual renaissance. Early in his life with Eli, we know that he literally heard God speak to him. Eli, in his wisdom, simply told Samuel to listen. Part of what Samuel heard was about Israel's coming defeat at the hands of the Philistines, and how the enemy would capture the sacred Ark of the Covenant. Samuel shared all this information with Eli, including the fact that Eli's two sons would be killed in the battle (see 1 Sam. 3:11-21).

As Samuel grew, he became well known and more and more highly respected by the people. Over time, he gradually took over Eli's duties as the priest in Israel, and when Eli died, he became the replacement. He was also referred to as a prophet. He was also their military leader. So he had those three roles in his relationship with Israel. He was such a powerful figure in Israel's relationship with God that when God was speaking to Jeremiah about the Israelites, he said, "Even if Moses and Samuel stood before me pleading for these people, I wouldn't help them" (Jer. 15:1).

The Philistines thought they had captured the God of Israel when they captured the Ark. But after their god Dagon was destroyed by the presence of the Ark, and after several plagues hit each town where the Ark was kept, the Philistines returned the Ark to Israel. At this time, Samuel challenged the people to a spiritual awakening. He told them to get rid of their foreign gods and to "determine to obey only the LORD" (1 Sam. 7:3). The people did what he asked, and repented. And then Samuel did what he loved to do. He gathered the people together at Mizpah for a meeting. During that meeting, the Philistines launched an attack on Israel, but God intervened and the Israelites subdued the Philistines. For a number of years, they didn't bother Israel. And during that time, "Samuel continued as Israel's judge for the rest of his life" (v. 15).

What We Often Overlook

Israel had been waiting, and remember that even though they didn't know it at the time, they were waiting for a king. At this point in the narrative, Samuel's story becomes woven in with Saul's story, and then blends in with the beginning of David's story. All this was set in motion while Israel still waited for a king. With that passing of time, Samuel grew older, and he finally appointed his sons to be judges over Israel. We read, "They were not like their father, for they were greedy for money. They accepted bribes and perverted justice" (1 Sam. 8:3).

It's interesting to note that Samuel's family dynamics were a continuation of Eli's family dynamics. He obviously had little contact with his birth parents, for his own family resembled Eli's family, not Elkanah's family. Eli had two sons who were wicked, and Samuel had two sons who were even more wicked. In fact, like all dysfunctional patterns in families, Samuel's sons went even further in their wickedness than Eli's sons. They actually directly violated the teachings of God given by Moses. They had no concept of true justice!

At this point, Israel had tasted what justice looked like, and they didn't want anything to do with Samuel's two sons, so they confronted Samuel and said, "Give us a king to judge us like all the other nations have" (v. 5). Samuel was not very happy with this request. He went before God, and as he presented the case, he was feeling sorry for God. It is more likely that he was really feeling sorry for himself. But he masked it. God wasn't upset by this request for a king, for He knew this day would come. Moses predicted this day when he gave his final sermon to Israel. He said:

> You are about to enter the land the LORD your God is giving you. When you take it over and settle there, you may think, "We should select a king to rule over us like the other nations around us." If this happens, be sure to select as king the man the LORD your God chooses. You must appoint a fellow Israelite; he may not be a foreigner (Deut. 17:14-15).

Then Moses went on to describe how the king should behave. There is no indication in the passage that suggests God would be displeased when a king was chosen. In fact, Moses used the exact words the elders of Israel used when they said to Samuel—"like the other nations around us." In fact, Hannah, in her prophetic prayer of praise, even predicted that Israel would have a king (see 1 Sam. 2:10). So it is clear that God wasn't blindsided by what the elders of Israel were asking for.

But Samuel was displeased; and I believe that was for several reasons. First, he was displeased because he was blind to his own sons' sinful activities. He didn't see the problem. To Samuel, they weren't as bad as the people were saying. After all, they were his sons—he knew their hearts. They were really good boys, and they would come around. Second, the idea of a king was not a part of Samuel's vision for Israel. After all, things were working well right now. A king would only mess things up. Let's stick with judges and priests. Perhaps that's part of why Samuel, not God, was offended by the elders' request. God could see through the mask designed by Samuel to hide his hurt at the elders' rejection of his sons, but God told Samuel to go ahead and grant the elders their request.

Samuel was not about to give up. He went back to the elders and harshly criticized the idea of a king. He pointed out all the oppressive things that would happen with a king (see 1 Sam. 8:10-18).

Six times he told them what the king would take from them. He would "take" your daughters, the best of your fields, a tenth of your grain and grape harvest, your male and female slaves, the finest of your cattle and donkeys. He would take your sons and draft them into the military, while others would be drafted into his work force. Then he told them they would someday beg for relief from the king's demands, but God wouldn't help them in that day.

Samuel's words fell on deaf ears as the elders repeated their request for a king. Again, Samuel went before the Lord as if to get God to agree with him and deny the request. But once again, God said, "Do as they say, and give them a king" (1 Sam. 8:21). Samuel gave in and sent the people home.

Later on, when young Saul comes to Samuel to ask for help in finding his father's donkeys, God had already told Samuel that at a certain time on a certain day, the man God had chosen to be king would appear before him. And Saul appeared at that moment. He was the man God had chosen.

Samuel was very gracious with Saul, providing food and shelter and then, in the morning, anointed him to be king. Samuel then told Saul that this would be confirmed on his way home. He told Saul three things that would happen to him, and each happened as Samuel had predicted.

Of course, there was to be a public announcement about Saul. So once again, Samuel called all of Israel to a meeting at Mizpah. He went through the process of choosing by casting lots, first the tribe of Benjamin—the smallest tribe; then the larger family was chosen; then the family of Kish was chosen. Finally it was announced that Saul was to be king. Israel now had moved from the chaos of the time of the judges to what they hoped would be the security of a king.

Samuel's defensive attitude can be seen several more times. In 1 Samuel 12, he gave his farewell speech, and once again we see his dislike for the idea of a king. Samuel asks the people, "Whose ox or donkey have I stolen? Have I ever cheated any of you? Have I ever oppressed you? Have I ever taken a bribe and perverted justice?" (1 Sam. 12:3). And each time the answer was, "No, Samuel you never did that." But the answer could have been, "No, Samuel, you never did that, but your sons did." He also pointed out that both the people and the king now had a responsibility to fear and worship the Lord, and if they did, all would be well with Israel. But his speech was motivated in part by his bitterness over the rejection of his two sons by the people.

We also see Samuel's internal fight against the idea of a king when Saul asks Samuel to come and offer a sacrifice before they are to go into battle with the Philistines. Samuel told him he would be there in seven days to offer the sacrifice. But as the seventh day passed with no Samuel, the men became restless, with some even starting to head for home, believing that God wasn't going to be in this battle. Things were falling apart, so Saul, as the king, and as their leader, took it upon himself to sacrifice the burnt offering on his own. Just as he finished, Samuel appeared and confronted Saul over his offering the sacrifice.

Some say this is when God removed his blessing from Saul; but I don't think that fits the text of the Bible. In God's eyes, Saul's offering the sacrifice wasn't a problem. After all, if later on, David, who had no priestly role, could offer a burnt offering sacrifice and a peace offering when the Ark was returned to Jerusalem; or if he could eat the bread on the Table of the Presence, which was reserved only for the priests, and God didn't rebuke him, what limited Saul as king from filling this priestly role under these important circumstances? There are other examples of one of Israel's kings offering a sacrifice. Solomon is one (see 1 Kings 3:15; 8:64), and King Ahaz (see 2 Kings 16:12-13). Even Gideon, as a judge, offered a burnt offering sacrifice (see Judg. 6:26). It seems that the only commandment Saul violated was the one that he held to, "Thou shalt not violate Samuel's authority."

Here's what I think was going on. Samuel was bitter, and he still resented the fact that God allowed Israel to have a king instead of allowing his sons to judge Israel. When Saul asked him to come and offer the sacrifice before the battle, part of Samuel didn't want to do it; but another part of Samuel knew it was right that he do it.

There is a thing called "passive resistance," which describes behavior when a part of us doesn't want to do something, We may passively resist doing it. We get busy with other things. We forget what time we agreed on. We are delayed in getting somewhere. Somehow we're just always late because of our passive resistance. Now, if someone is late for an appointment once, not a problem. Passive resistance is usually the case when someone is habitually late.

We don't know that Samuel was habitually late with Saul, as there is nothing in the Bible that suggests that. But with something as important as this appointment was to Saul, it seems to me that this is an example of Samuel passively resisting an important opportunity to fully support Saul.

Without diminishing in any way the greatness of Samuel, I think he took his time getting to where Saul was, and he may even have been standing on a hillside nearby waiting and watching to see what Saul was going to do. He waited long enough for Saul to take things into his own hands and save the day with his troops. Saul was surprised by Samuel's reaction. He explained, "I saw my men scattering from me, and you didn't arrive when you said you would, and the Philistines are at Micmash ready for battle. So I said, 'The Philistines are ready to march against us at Gilgal, and I haven't even asked for the LORD's help!' So I felt compelled to offer the burnt offering myself before you came" (1 Sam. 13:11-12). The evidence in favor of Saul's position on all this is that the Israelites prevailed in the ensuing battle. God didn't punish Saul. Instead, he rewarded him with a victory.

Saul does lose the anointing of God, but that comes later, in 1 Samuel 15, and this time Samuel is right on. Saul was instructed to destroy the Amalekites—the entire nation! No one was to survive, and even all property, including the animals, was to be destroyed. Saul took his army of 210,000 men and destroyed "most" of the nation of the Amalekites—not "all" as he had been instructed. As he returned home, God told Samuel what had happened and that He was "sorry that I ever made Saul king, for he has not been loyal to me and has refused to obey my command" (1 Sam. 15:11). Apparently, Samuel was now on board with this king idea, and he was deeply upset when God told him this. In his distress, he cried out to the Lord on behalf of Saul all night long.

Early in the morning, Samuel went looking for Saul. When he found him, Saul was in a great mood, but Samuel was deeply saddened. He confronted Saul with the evidence that not everything and everyone was destroyed. He asked Saul, "What is all the bleating of sheep and goats and the lowing of cattle I hear?" (v. 14). When Saul tried to rationalize what he had done, Samuel makes that great statement that "obedience is better than sacrifice" (v. 22). But notice also the context of that powerful statement. Samuel told Saul, "What is more pleasing to the LORD: your burnt offerings and sacrifices or your obedience to his voice? Listen! Obedience is better than sacrifice, and submission is better than offering the fat of rams. Rebellion is as sinful as witchcraft, and stubbornness as bad as worshiping idols" (vv. 22-23). This time, God's anointing on Saul was removed.

As a result, Samuel had one more special task to do, and that was to anoint the next king. This time, God told him the specific family. He said, "Go to Bethlehem. Find a man named Jesse who lives there" (1 Sam. 16:1). Samuel feared for his life, fearing that Saul would seek to kill him. So God suggested he take a heifer and say that he was going to Bethlehem to offer a sacrifice. When he arrived in Bethlehem, the elders were afraid, wondering why he was there. Apparently this wasn't one of his regular stops in his role as judge. He reassured them and then found the family of Jesse. In the privacy of the family, Samuel told them the real reason he was there. So the family gathered for the "sacrifice," and Samuel started to size up the sons. To him, they all appeared to be "kingly" material; but much to Samuel's surprise, none of them was chosen by the Lord.

Oops! They forgot one of their sons! The youngest was out in the fields and was completely forgotten by his dad! Samuel told them to send for him, and when he walked in, God told Samuel, "This is the one; anoint him" (v. 12). The waiting was over; the king Israel had been waiting for had arrived. And though Samuel continued to act as judge until his death, we hear no more about this great man until the statement, "Now Samuel died, and all Israel gathered for his funeral. They buried him at his house in Ramah" (1 Sam. 25:1). His task for God was finished. But his death also marked the return of the Philistines as a menace to Israel and her king.

So What Can We Learn?

One of the themes in the story of Samuel is the theme of waiting. Israel was waiting for a king; Hannah was waiting for a son. We don't know how many years passed from the end of the book of Judges until we meet Hannah and Elkanah, but they were years during which God was silent. In the silence of God, Israel failed miserably. When finally, God intervened and opened Hannah's womb, and Samuel was born, things slowly began to change. The goal wasn't what Samuel wanted, and it probably wasn't what God wanted. But it was what the people wanted once they got things right in their relationship with God. So the waiting was over, and God granted their desire for a king.

But how did Israel wait? In their waiting, they failed miserably. They rejected God and became gods unto themselves. "They did whatever seemed right in their own eyes." They also worshipped the gods of the surrounding people, something God had Moses warn them about repeatedly. No, they didn't wait well. The waiting periods in life are always a test of trust. The Israelites put their trust in themselves and in their idols made with human hands. To us that may look foolish. How can you trust something that someone else created? But don't we do the same thing? We put our trust in how much money we have, the people to whom we are connected, our job. As long as these things are working, we feel like everything is okay. Maybe we don't see these things as idols, but they represent where we are putting our trust.

The second problem the Israelites experienced while waiting was that they stopped listening to God's voice. The early judges had a strong spiritual foundation. They listened to God. But the later judges listened less and less, until it appeared that God was silent. Maybe He wasn't silent—maybe they just stopped listening, at least to God. Instead, they listened to their own desires. They only trusted themselves.

When we trust someone, we listen to that person. The problem in Samuel's day, and before Samuel, was that no one was listening to God. Samuel changed all of that. He was a listener. Remember that story of the teacher who read the story of Eli and Samuel to her second grade class? Early in his relationship with Eli, Samuel was awakened at night by a voice calling out "Samuel!" Samuel ran to Eli, thinking that it was him calling. Three times this happened, and each time Samuel heard the voice and responded. Finally, Eli recognized that it was God calling Samuel, and told him how to respond. He told him to simply say, "Speak, LORD, your servant is listening" (1 Sam. 3:9). So Samuel did just that—he listened! And God gave him an earful about what was going to happen in Israel.

The word used for "listen" in the original language means more than to simply hear. It also includes the idea of obeying what you hear. This becomes clearer when you look at Samuel's farewell speech to the Israelites. He put forth the following proposition:

> Now if you fear and worship the LORD and listen to his voice, and if you do not rebel against the LORD's commands, then both you and your king will show that you recognize the LORD as your God. But if you rebel against the LORD's commands and refuse to listen to him, then his hand will be as heavy upon you as it was upon your ancestors (1 Sam. 12:14-15).

Samuel used the word "listen" twice—in the positive sense and in the negative sense. His proposition could easily be paraphrased, "Now if you fear and worship the Lord, and hear, listen to, and obey his voice . . ." That was the meaning of "to listen" to the Hebrews.

Samuel was setting it up for the people in as clear a way as possible. He was also stating why he didn't think they needed a king, for the future was not dependent on the king. He stated clearly that it depended on both the people and the king listening and obeying the Lord God. This was true for the Israelites, and it is just as true for us today. While Samuel was speaking to Israel about their history, the writer of Hebrews refers to that same period of time as a warning to us. He says, "Today when you hear his voice, don't harden your hearts as Israel did when they rebelled, when they tested me in the wilderness" (Heb. 3:7-8). Instead: *Listen!*

But how do we listen? It isn't easy in today's crowded world. God speaks to us in many ways. For starters, He speaks to us through His Word, the Scriptures. Sometimes we think that means that we can open the Bible and point to a verse and assume that God is speaking to our situation. That sometimes happens, but that's not the disciplined way of actually hearing God. We need to go beyond looking at the words on the page of the Bible. We need to get the Word of God into our hearts. It's like planting the seed of God's Word within us, so that over time it can sprout and bear fruit—especially in the waiting periods of our lives. The psalmist tells us, "I have hidden your word in my heart, that I might not sin against you" (Ps. 119:11).

We also hear God through other believers. Hannah heard God speak to her through the words of Eli the priest. When she heard him say to her, "Go in peace! May the God of Israel grant the request you have asked of him" (1 Sam. 1:17), she took his words as the words of God and literally went in peace. She got her appetite back and began to eat again. She heard and she believed. In the same way, Samuel listened to Eli when he was told how to answer the voice that was calling him in the night.

But as we will see when we look at Elijah, God also speaks to us in the quiet moments of life—in that still small voice within us. We are often so busy that we never hear the whispers of God within. We think it's our own voice, or something we heard someone else say somewhere.

A friend was driving and heard in his heart the words, "You have not, because you ask not." The words seemed to just come out of nowhere. But as he meditated on the words, he thought of the chronic pain he continually experienced, and so he asked God to take the pain away. To his amazement, the pain left, never to return. When we think that God doesn't speak to us, the truth is, we aren't listening. Slow down and listen. See what you hear in God's whispers.

Regardless of what we hear or don't hear—regardless of how we listen—God is seeking to communicate with us. We do not have a silent God, even when we think He is silent. We need to say with Samuel, "Speak, Lord, for your servant is listening."

The "Could Have Been" Saint

Yes, I have sinned. I have disobeyed your instructions and the LORD's command, for I was afraid of the people and did what they demanded.
1 SAMUEL 15:24

Some years ago, I was listening to a speaker talk about how tenuously some of us hold on to our beliefs. He made a statement that I have never forgotten. He said that too many of us willingly change what we believe in order to fit our beliefs to our behavior. I must have been young and naïve, because that statement shocked me. I thought to myself, *That can't be! He must have it backwards. If someone believes something, that will affect the way they behave; not the other way around.* But over the years, as I've worked with people, both as a pastor and as a counselor, I have found it to be true. People change their beliefs to fit their behavior.

Apparently we place what we believe into three categories. We have our public beliefs, which are things we are "supposed" to believe. We believe them because we are Americans, or because we are Baptists or Presbyterians or Pentecostals. Or, they may represent what we think we are supposed to believe based on which political party we identify with. We can state these public beliefs, but they typically are merely words.

Then there are our private beliefs. We hold these a little closer. These may be things we learned in our family or in the church where we are members, and we think we really hold to these truths. They may be values and beliefs that we think we hold to strongly, like our position on abortion. But when push comes to shove, we can temporarily set aside what we believe when it contradicts what we are about to do.

I worked with a family that was very active in the pro-life movement. They were leaders in their church's involvement in the movement. Anyone who knew them had no doubts about their position—they were firmly and absolutely opposed to abortion. But then their teenage daughter got pregnant by a boyfriend they didn't like, and suddenly the family became divided as the parents pushed for an abortion, and the siblings of the pregnant girl fought to uphold their family's pro-life beliefs. The abortion took place and ended up dividing the family. Their private beliefs, which seemed so strong, suddenly changed in order to fit what they were going to do. Apparently there was more at stake in this unwanted pregnancy for the parents than for the siblings, for they changed their beliefs to fit their behavior!

The third category describes our core beliefs. If we typically give only lip service to our public beliefs, and only hold a little more strongly to our private beliefs, then our core beliefs are what we would call our "non-negotiables." These we won't change. They are the ones that ultimately determine our behavior. In fact, we can define our core beliefs by looking at our behavior. These core beliefs also form part of what we call character. What are we willing to die for? The answer to that question tells us a lot about who we are—what our basic character is. And when we come to the character of King Saul, we may be surprised by his core beliefs and what he would call his non-negotiables.

What We Know

Saul appeared during Israel's "waiting" scene, and people assumed the waiting was then over. They had a king. But as we will see, he was just a transition between the period of the judges and the king that would define Israel, King David. I believe God planned that Saul would be more than a transition, but Saul had a lot to do with that outcome.

When we first meet Saul, he is a young man on a mission. His father had sent him, along with a servant, to find some lost donkeys. Their determination to find the donkeys tells us something about Saul's relationship with his father. Tradition suggests that Kish, Saul's father, was a general in the Israelite army. Perhaps he ran his home as if it were a boot camp, and Saul and the servant were a couple of new recruits.

Author Pat Conroy has written a number of novels, one of which is *The Great Santini*, whose main character is based on Conroy's father. He was literally the pilot the Marine Corps called the "Great Santini." Colonel Conroy did run his family of boys as if they were raw Marine recruits and he was their drill sergeant. He wasn't a very loving father, for that would reflect softness, and he believed a Marine colonel cannot be soft, even at home. Neither could a general, such as Saul's father. So maybe Saul's boyhood was similar to Pat Conroy's boyhood—filled with fear, criticism and judgment.

As you read the story about Saul, it seems clear that Saul and his servant—especially the servant—were afraid to go home without finding the donkeys. After all, Saul and the servant were given a task to do, and there was no such thing as failure! After three days, though, Saul was ready to give up and go home. He had a new fear, which he identified when he said, "By now my father will be more worried about us than about the donkeys!" (1 Sam. 9:5). But the servant wasn't ready to go home just yet. He had one more option. He said, "I've just thought of something! There is a man of God who lives here in this town. He is held in high honor by all the people because everything he says comes true. Let's go find him. Perhaps he can tell us which way to go" (v. 6). And that brought Saul into the presence of Samuel.

As we continue the story of Saul, we will see that his fear-based approach to life becomes even clearer. When Samuel anointed him with oil and told him he was going to be the ruler over Israel, Saul didn't know what to make of it. Certainly he heard the words, even though he said nothing. When Samuel called all the people to gather at Mizpah in order to choose a king, Saul knew it was going to be him. So what happened? After Samuel went through the casting of lots to first determine which tribe, and then which clan, and then the specific family, it was announced that Saul, the son of Kish, was the king. You would think that Saul would reluctantly stand up and then slowly come to the front of the crowd—all to the cheers of the people. But not fearful Saul. When Samuel announced Saul's name, there was probably silence as everyone waited. Then a low murmur began to fill the valley as people turned to each other, trying to understand what was taking place.

There was no Saul to come to the front of the crowd! They knew he was there, so they looked for him. But they couldn't find him. Finally, Samuel asked the Lord, "Where is he?" and the Lord said, "He is hiding among the baggage" (1 Sam. 10:22). This fearful young man, who stood head and shoulders taller than anyone, was the king, and he was hiding! Now why would he hide when he knew he would be picked? He was obviously trying to protect himself from what he perceived to be a threatening situation. Fearful people run from challenges. Fearful people do not want to meet life head-on; they'd rather hide. Some might see this as modesty. But the modest person is willing to accept challenges. The rabbinical stories said that the real reason Saul failed was that he was too mild mannered, which they saw as a major problem for a ruler. Either way—too mild, or too fearful, Saul obviously didn't really want this job.

When Saul came out of hiding, even Samuel seemed to be impressed with his appearance. "Samuel said to all the people, 'This is the man the LORD has chosen as your king. No one in all Israel is like him!' And all the people shouted, 'Long live the king!'" (v. 24). That was quite a recommendation—no one like him in all of Israel!

But there were some in the crowd who saw things differently. They are referred to in the text as "scoundrels," but they were also realists. They said to each other, "Our new king knows he is going to be chosen, and during the time of choosing, he is hiding?" So they legitimately asked "How can this man save us?" (v. 27). And, like the fearful young man that he was, we read that "Saul ignored them." He wasn't about to confront anyone. And then everyone went home, including Saul.

There was no palace for him to live in. There was no crown that he was supposed to wear. In fact, for some time, nothing in Saul's life really changed. He simply went back to work plowing his father's fields. He probably thought to himself, *So what's the big deal? I'm supposed to be king, but here I am plowing. Don't really know what I was afraid of.* But all that was soon to change.

About this time, King Nahash of Ammon set up a siege around the Israelite city of Jabesh-gilead. People couldn't leave, and no supplies could be brought in. It was a method of warfare that simply wore down the enemy. When the citizens realized there was nothing they could do, they were ready to capitulate. King Nahash's condition for releasing the city was that everyone's right eye was to be gouged out. The Bible says this was to be a humiliation against Israel, but it was also a common practice of that period of time. If you lost an eye, you were no longer any good as a soldier. You lost your depth perception, so you really didn't know where to throw your spear. Obviously, it was a cruel time to be alive. It's hard for us to imagine that this was a common practice. The king was so certain that he had won, he gave the people of Jabesh-gilead seven days to see if they could find help. So they sent word of their plight throughout Israel.

When the messengers from Jabesh-gilead arrived in Saul's village, he was out in the fields plowing. All the people were distraught when he came in from his field, and he asked what was happening. When they told him about their kinsmen in Jabesh-gilead, a remarkable thing happened. It says that "The Spirit of God came powerfully upon Saul, and he became very angry" (1 Sam. 11:6). The infilling of the Holy Spirit gave Saul the ability to experience his anger. As a result, he cut up two oxen, gave each person a piece and sent them throughout Israel saying that this would happen to their oxen if they didn't come and follow Saul into battle. The people came, they went to Jabesh and they defeated King Nahash and his army. They freed the citizens. Now Saul was celebrated as king by everyone for he had done the very thing that led the people to want a king—he had protected them! And so they had another solemn ceremony where they reaffirmed Saul as their king. When some suggested that they now kill those who mocked him earlier, like the leader he had become, he said, "No one will be executed today, for today the LORD has rescued Israel!" (1 Sam. 11:13).

What We Often Overlook

Why the change in Saul? Obviously, something miraculous had taken place in him. To understand it, we have to understand something about how fear-based people operate. As I said earlier, when someone lives as a fearful person, he or she avoids an unusual or unknown situation, and seldom gets angry. The reason is that fear and anger are opposite emotions. You can't experience them at the same time. For example, imagine that you are visiting a friend who lives in a very dangerous part of town. You arrive quite late in the evening and you have to park several blocks away. It's dark, and as you start to walk toward your friend's apartment, you hear footsteps behind you. You start walking faster, and the footsteps behind you speed up as well. You're too afraid to stop and look back, so you start running. So does the person behind you. And as you knock on your friend's front door, you discover the footsteps following you belong to your friend when he laughs and says, "I got you!" Now your fear has vanished and you're angry at the mean trick your former friend just pulled on you!

How long did it take for your fear to turn to anger? A split second. Once your perception of what appeared to be threatening wasn't a threat, you felt anger. So both fear and anger, when experienced in the here-and-now of life, are based on your perceptions.

If the threat is big and scary, you feel fear. If what you thought was a threat turns out not to be a threat, you feel angry.

When you grow up, as Saul probably did, in a continual state of fear, you don't often, if ever, get angry—certainly not at home. Anger was probably seen as rebellion. Saul's growing-up experiences had left a fear-wound in Saul, and we see the effect of that wound when he is afraid to go home, and especially when he, knowing he is to be chosen as king, hides among the people's baggage.

The miracle is that God instantly healed him of his fear-based pattern. When Saul heard about the plight of the people of Jabesh-gilead, under normal circumstances he would have grieved with his fellow villagers. But he was the king, and the people wanted a king for just a time as this. God knew Saul's potential, so he sent the Holy Spirit to come powerfully upon Saul, and the evidence of the infilling of the Holy Spirit was that Saul "burned with anger!" (1 Sam. 11:6, *NIV*). Prior to this, he was like Jacob. He was able to love, but he wasn't able to be angry. Instead of the anger, he experienced fear. But with the healing of his emotional wound, Saul was now a balanced man and became a powerful leader. God knew what He was doing when He chose Saul!

There are some today who say that God purposely picked a loser to be the king in order to show the people they shouldn't have wanted a king. But we know that God doesn't act in that way. He doesn't make a mistake in order to teach us something. He just doesn't make mistakes. And the choice of Saul was not a mistake. He had the potential to be a great leader. Look at his life. He obviously was a great family man. Unlike David, he had just one wife. And unlike David, his children were loyal to him to the day he died. He had a strong, loyal, powerful son in Jonathan. And the people loved him. If Saul hadn't blown it, he could have been the pivotal personality of the Old Testament; or if not him, certainly his son Jonathan would have been so. The rabbis point out that even before being chosen king, Saul was a military hero. He was handsome, and to use their words, he had "unusual beauty." But he was also exceedingly modest, even what might be called naive and innocent. And unlike what would happen with David, his troops never rebelled against him. They were always loyal. He was a solid citizen of Israel.

The rabbis even want to defend Saul, for they say, "Compared with David's sins, Saul's were not sufficiently grievous to account for the withdrawal of the royal dignity from him and his family."[1] So why was his anointing, his blessing, withdrawn? It still has a lot to do with his fear.

In the previous chapter, we looked at the first confrontation between Samuel and Saul, found in 1 Samuel 13. But we looked at it from Samuel's side; so now let's look at it from Saul's perspective. When someone is afraid of his or her father, or has issues with him, one of the struggles he or she will have in life has to do with their attitude toward authority figures. In the home, dad is considered the authority figure, whether he likes it or not, and whether he acts on it or not. That's how children perceive their father. If he abuses his role as father in any way, this then gets transferred to his children's relationship with any authority figure—policemen, bosses, anyone who in some way has authority over them.

For Saul, Samuel was an authority figure. Even though Saul was the king, Samuel had been the leader and was still highly respected throughout Israel. And Samuel treated Saul in a way that reminded Saul that in many ways, Samuel was still the boss. God spoke to Saul through Samuel—to Saul, that alone gave Samuel authority.

When Samuel didn't show up on time to offer the sacrifice, Saul saw no problem with going ahead and offering the sacrifice himself. He probably knew that Gideon had acted in this priestly way, and he saw no reason why he couldn't do the same. After all, the stakes were high, and they were growing. Already, too many of his troops had given up and gone home. They didn't want to fight if God wasn't going to be involved with them in the battle. In fact, when Saul finally went to battle, he had only 600 troops left.

But when Samuel challenged Saul, it was as if he had opened that old father wound in Saul. Saul was taken aback and probably began to question himself about what he had done. He didn't know that whatever rule he had broken was simply one of Samuel's commandments, not God's. Samuel was not only seen as an authority figure, but he was also, literally, the voice of God to Saul. It was like Samuel and God were all mixed together in Saul's mind. We saw earlier that Samuel had his own set of problems. But Saul was too close to it to see that in what had just happened.

Saul did go into battle, and with Jonathan's bravery and faith, they defeated the Philistines. Their victory should have been reassuring to Saul, but I think that when the battle was over, he could not get Samuel's words out of his mind. Instead of seeing the victory as evidence that God was still using and blessing him, he let his authority issues with Samuel erode his confidence, and this set him on a slippery slope that led to his ultimate failure.

Sometime later, Samuel came to Saul again and gave Saul his instructions for the destruction of the Amalekites. Everything and everyone was to be destroyed. There was to be no spoils of the battle. Now that's a tough one for the army. After all, the only way the soldiers in his army would get paid was for them to win the battle and take home what was left, the "spoils." The spoils were their pay. In fact, if you lost the battle, you became part of the spoils for the opposing army. You became their paycheck.

Saul knew what he was supposed to do, but he didn't do it. After the victory, they returned home with sheep, goats and cattle, and with the enemy king alive but captive. When you are a fear-based person, and you are confronted with something, you develop a skill at diverting the confrontation. And Saul was good at it. When Samuel confronted him, Saul immediately diverted the accusation with a "spiritual" response. He told Samuel, Oh yes, we brought them back because we "are going to sacrifice them to the LORD your God. We have destroyed everything else" (1 Sam. 15:15). He thought the spiritual nature of his answer would placate Samuel. But it didn't. Saul was full of excuses because Samuel was his "boss," and he knew he had done wrong. But it would take some time for him to finally admit it.

When Saul finally admitted that he had disobeyed, he mixed God and Samuel together. And then he told why he disobeyed. He said, "Yes, I have sinned. I have disobeyed your instructions and the LORD's command, for I was afraid of the people and did what they demanded" (1 Sam. 15:24). "I was afraid of the people!" What God had healed, as recorded in 1 Samuel 11, Saul had undone. He wasn't afraid when he went up against King Nahash. That was part of his healing. But in just a short time, Saul had undone the healing and was once again living in fear. But there was more to it.

Saul had to cover up his fear, even to himself. So he got caught up in his new image as king. In his confrontation with Samuel he was more concerned about his image before the people than he was about having disobeyed God. He begged Samuel to "forgive my sin." He didn't ask God to forgive him as David did when Nathan confronted him over his sin. He asked Samuel to forgive his sin, and then said "come back with me so that I may worship the LORD" (v. 25). When Samuel turned to walk away, Saul grabbed his robe and tore it, stopping Samuel. Again, he begged Samuel to "at least honor me before the elders of my people and before Israel by coming back with me so that I may worship the LORD your God" (v. 30). And Samuel agreed this time.

Because Saul had authority issues he struggled in his relationship with the Lord as well. Two times, in talking with Samuel, he referred to God as "the LORD your God." He didn't say the LORD *my* God, or *our* God. What this indicates is that now Saul was totally dependent on himself and was concerned only about his image. He wanted to look good before the people. Unlike his giving credit to God for defeating King Nahash, now God wasn't even on his radar. And that's why I think the verse reads, "The LORD was sorry he had ever made Saul king of Israel" (v. 35).

More of What We Know

When the Spirit of God left Saul at the end of 1 Samuel 15, "a tormenting spirit . . . filled him with depression and fear" (1 Sam. 16:14). The text literally says, "the tormenting spirit from God troubled Saul" (1 Sam. 16:23), or as the *King James Version* puts it, "when the evil spirit from God was upon Saul," David would play his harp for Saul. How can an evil spirit come from God? We have trouble with this concept, but the people of Israel didn't seem to worry about such a thing. They had a monotheistic understanding of God, who did everything. He did good, and he could do evil. Amos asks, "Shall there be evil in a city, and the LORD hath not done it?" (Amos 3:6, *KJV*). Our best way of understanding this wording is to say that it was as if God had given Saul over to his fears.

His deepening fears were a reaction to his confrontation with Samuel and the realization that he had completely blown everything. The kingdom was taken from him, which meant not only his loss but also his son Jonathan's loss, for he was next in line to be king. In his deep fearfulness and despair Saul thought the only solution was to get rid of David, and this became the primary focus of the remainder of Saul's life.

This is also where the story shifts to David as the main character. And as Saul interacted with David his fears deepened. Regardless of what David did, Saul was convinced that David intended to kill him. After all, if you thought like Saul, with no regard for the divine perspective, you would have done exactly what Saul tried to do—kill David. In Saul's way of thinking David must have wanted to kill him so that he could be king. And Saul wouldn't let go of that idea, even though twice David could have killed him, but didn't. As you read through the rest of 1 Samuel, you see that Saul was obsessed with David. He spent all his energy trying to find him; but God never allowed Saul to succeed. When Saul was searching for David there were times when the Philistines started to harass the Israelites, so that Saul had to break off his obsession with David and go deal with the enemy. But in truth, the rest of the book of 1 Samuel is about David. Saul is just a sidebar.

We read that following Samuel's confrontation with Saul their relationship ended. From that day forward, Samuel never met with Saul again. But Saul missed Samuel, and the rabbis say that no one felt the death of Samuel more than did Saul. This is clear when Saul consulted the witch of Endor before what would prove to be his final battle. Samuel, the prophet of the Lord, was dead. And

God had stopped communicating with Saul. So he had the witch of Endor conjure up the ghost of Samuel so that he could consult with him about the upcoming battle. Saul had outlawed witchcraft in Israel, but he was desperate to talk with Samuel. Saul had no one to turn to—he was alone. In order to consult the witch, Saul had to disguise himself so he wouldn't be recognized.

The rabbinical story about this event says that when the ghost of Samuel appeared he was standing upright, not upside down, not standing on his head. This only happened when the living person seeking to communicate with the dead was a king. This was their explanation for how the witch knew that it was King Saul who was before her. Samuel was upset that he was being disturbed. When Saul said he had to ask Samuel what to do because God didn't speak to him anymore through either a prophet or through a dream, Samuel told Saul that he and his three sons would die in the battle. It is to Saul's credit that he pulled himself together at the end of his life and died honorably. He went to war knowing that he would lose his life. It's as if he finally accepted the punishment that God had ordained for him.

So What Can We Learn?

Saul is one of the most tragic figures in all of Israel's history. The tragedy is the sadness about what he could have been. In many ways, he was a great leader. He had no problem with his soldiers or with his people—they were always loyal to him, even to the end of Saul's life. But his problems had a lot to do with how he arranged his three different belief systems. In regard to his public belief system, he fit in with what Israel stood for. He could act the part. He believed in God, and he was concerned about worshipping the Lord. But his public beliefs never really went very deep within Saul. Remember, he referred to God as the "LORD *your* God" several times, like a slip of the tongue that revealed his lack of personal commitment to Yahweh, the LORD. His relationship with God was superficial and at best was expressed in his life only through his relationship with Samuel.

His private beliefs probably had a lot to do with his family. Family was important to Saul, and he lived this out throughout his life. This is especially seen in his relationship with his son Jonathan. Although Jonathan was totally loyal to David as a friend, his loyalty to David was never at the expense of his relationship with his father. Even when Saul made that foolish oath before battling the Philistines—that anyone who eats before the battle must die—Jonathan didn't agree, but he was willing to accept what his father had set up. It was only the men of Saul's army who rescued Jonathan so that he wasn't put to death, arguing that Jonathan ate only because he didn't know about Saul's oath. Some of Saul's other private beliefs were similar to some of the pagan ideas of the people who surrounded Israel, which was an attempt to manipulate God in order to have victory.

We also see this private belief in his determined effort to kill David. It wasn't so much that David was going to replace him, but that David was going to replace his family—and replace Jonathan as the heir to the throne. Saul thought that if he could kill David, his lineage would be preserved and Jonathan would be the next king. Again, this belief didn't really include anything about what God planned, or what God wanted. It was all about what Saul wanted.

When you come to his core beliefs, you come to his major problem. At his core, Saul's belief system didn't truly include his relationship with God. Instead of developing his relationship with God, he relied on Samuel, and also on himself. In the place of reliance on God, Saul was more concerned about his image before the people than what God wanted from him. And it was this belief that eventually led to God's removing his anointing from Saul and giving it to David. Saul was desperate to have Samuel "worship" with him, which meant that there would be a sacrifice that Samuel would make with Saul at his side. But it wasn't so Saul could worship the Lord, it was so that he looked good to the elders and the people. He must look good at all costs—that was at the core of what he really believed.

And his confession of sin was superficial. His confession was primarily made to Samuel, and didn't really feel like it was a confession of sin before the Lord. It seemed to be simply a way to keep Samuel involved with him. There wasn't enough at the core of Saul for him to stand on his own in the strength of the Lord. Saul's life was about his image; his character seemed fragile—without a deep conviction within his soul.

This brings up the second point we can draw from the account of Saul. People often ask me why God doesn't just heal our emotional woundedness. After all, He has healed physical problems. But if we had an abusive parent or an absent, neglecting or rejecting parent, and that experience continues to affect our current relationships, why doesn't God just make it all better? It's a valid question, and I always direct the one who asks it to the story of Saul.

When the Spirit of the Lord came upon Saul, and he experienced his ability to be angry, God healed his woundedness. But Saul didn't nurture that healing, and as a result, the healing was wasted. There was no character development to accompany the healing. As a result, he moved from being an authentic person in 1 Samuel 11 back to the fearful person we saw in chapter 9 and would see again in chapter 15 and beyond. Why did he revert to his old ways? I say it is because he never learned the lessons that the "process" of healing would have provided him. Because he was healed in that instant, he never stopped long enough to understand and to experience the process. He just went on with life, which now was at the top of the heap. He was the king.

What is that healing process? Think what might have happened if Saul had opened himself to Samuel and said something like, "God may have picked me, but I'm not up for this. What do I do? How can I hear from the Lord? Would you walk alongside of me and tutor me in the ways of God?" If this had happened, Saul would have developed a godly belief system that would have strengthened his character development. It would have been written upon Saul's heart, and he would have continued to grow into an even more authentic man. I know that would have taken some adjustment on Samuel's part, but I think Samuel would have made that happen. If he had, we may not be talking today about the Davidic Covenant, or even seen or heard of David. Saul would have been a godly king, and he would have been followed by Jonathan, a man who already knew how to depend on God.

There were also two other obvious events where, if Saul had followed through, he could have experienced a deepening of his healing, at least as a man and as king, and maybe even spiritually. These two occasions were the times that David could have killed Saul, but didn't. (See 1 Samuel 24 and 26.) In the first event, as they shouted to each other across the open space between them, Saul wept as he said to David, "You are a better man than I am, for you have repaid me good for evil" (1 Sam. 24:17). He wept because he was facing the truth of his own life. If he had stayed with this truth, the authentic Saul could have emerged. But he didn't, instead giving in again to his fear and paranoia.

In the second situation, Saul confessed, "I have sinned. Come back home, my son, and I will no longer try to harm you, for you valued my life today. I have been a fool and very, very wrong" (1 Sam. 26:21). Again, Saul chose not to be who he really wanted to be and needed to be. If Saul had followed through on either of these statements, the healing of his life would have deepened. But he didn't. David knew he wouldn't. Saul leaves the scene after this second encounter with David. He only returns when he seeks for the ghost of Samuel, and when he dies in battle. The continuing confrontation with David is finally over. Saul fades from the scene and David takes center stage.

The healing process would have built character in Saul. That process always deepens our core beliefs and makes them more an integral part of who we are. Saul missed these opportunities, as he also missed in the earlier ones with Samuel. We don't want to be a Saul. We don't want to miss what God wants to teach us as He heals us.

I talked with a man after I had taught a group on some of these thoughts on Saul. He said to me, "I'm a Saul. And I'm hopelessly doomed to be a Saul." I stopped him and said, "No one needs to be a Saul. Saul chose to be who he was, and you have the same choice. If you think your experience is like Saul's, just wait until you see in the next chapter how bad David was. But he made different choices, and so he was not a Saul. In fact, David, in spite of his sinfulness, was "a man after God's own heart." There is healing available to each of us, and that healing process will build character in us. It doesn't make us perfect; it simply opens us to God's activity in our lives.

11

The Sinful Saint

But God removed Saul and replaced him with David, a man
about whom God said, "I have found David son of Jesse, a man
after my own heart. He will do everything I want him to do."

ACTS 13:22

I was having coffee with a pastor friend of mine, and we got to talking about King David. I told him I was about to write this chapter on David, and I was struggling with it. I wanted to be honest about David's life, but what God said about him didn't add up for me. How could God say that David was "a man after my own heart?" I mean, how does that fit in with David's affair with Bathsheba, or with his setting up her husband Uriah to be murdered? I know God forgave him, but weren't there consequences that affected their relationship? My pastor friend raised his own concerns. He reminded me about all those concubines David kept, and the seven wives he already had when he made Bathsheba his eighth wife. "What does God do with all of that?" he asked. We had an interesting conversation as we tried to fit all of this into our sense of how God viewed David.

David represents an interesting blending of both the good and the bad in a person. He was able to use his emotions and his senses to convey to us important truths, not only about himself, but also about the nature and character of God. This is clearly seen in his Psalms, as well as in his lament of the death of Saul and Jonathan. When we are struggling with our lives, we take comfort in the ways David described his struggles. There is no question about the "good" David. But when David's emotions clearly crossed the line when it came to wives and concubines and murder, how does that fit into his being a man after God's own heart?

Well, we had a great conversation, and some of what we discussed is in this chapter. And I knew I had to be honest about David's "bad" side, otherwise he isn't a real personality for us. So hang on as we try to find the balance between his goodness and his badness, and still see him as a saint—although he was, like us, a sinful saint.

What We Know

History, sermons, Sunday School lessons; all like to emphasize David's good side, with the exception of his affair with Bathsheba. The most familiar story about David is his confident confrontation of the Philistine giant named Goliath. Almost everyone knows that story. As a young man who was so small he didn't even fit into King Saul's armor, David faced the fearsome Goliath with only a slingshot and five stones—and with his strong belief that no one should "defy the armies of the living God" (1 Sam. 17:26). David's bravery was also motivated by his conviction that no one should defy Yahweh, the Living God—the LORD. This was a conviction he carried with him throughout his lifetime.

We're also familiar with the account of how Samuel came to Jesse's family to anoint the next king. But none of Jesse's sons were God's choice, and that left Samuel confused. He asked if there were any other sons, and Jesse remembered that he had a son who was out in the fields taking care of the sheep. David's father had forgotten about him. How strange! The ancient rabbis thought it was strange also, and they had an interesting explanation for this.

They said that in spite of Jesse's relationship with God, one of his female slaves caught his fancy. "He would have entered into illicit relations with her had his wife, Nazbat ... not frustrated the plan. She disguised herself as the slave, and Jesse, deceived by the ruse, met his own wife. The child born to Nazbat was given out as the son of the freed slave, so that the father might not discover the deception practiced upon him. This child was David."[1] According to this rabbinical interpretation, Jesse had what he thought of as an illicit sexual relationship with a slave woman who got pregnant. The child was his, but not in the same way as his other sons, since he was born to a slave woman—the result of an affair.

The rabbis go on to say that because David was presumed to be the child of that slave, he was not considered to be fully one of Jesse's sons—and that's what Jesse thought, for he did not yet know the truth about David's birth-mother.

When Samuel anointed David, and all were amazed that the son of a slave woman should be made king, it was then that Nazbat revealed her secret to everyone and acknowledged that David was the rightful son who had been born to her and Jesse. Obviously, the rabbis were also trying to understand and explain how a father could forget about a son!

We know through reading the Psalms the terror of the years that King Saul hunted David down with the intent to kill him. Saul knew that Samuel had already anointed David as the next king, and Saul was determined that there would be no King David in the future. He was serious about eliminating the threat to the lineage of his own family. Many of David's psalms were written during this horrible period of his life as he and his band of followers hid in the wilderness. Yet, through all of that, David was loyal to Saul; and even though he had two opportunities to kill Saul, he refused to do so. He would not lay hands on "God's anointed one."

We're also familiar with David's military prowess. We saw this in his defeat of Goliath. David was feared by Israel's enemy, the Philistines. Part of Saul's problem with David was his jealousy of David's military success. He never could get over the song that the women sang celebrating one of David's victories over the

Philistines. They sang, "Saul has killed his thousands, and David his ten thousands!" (1 Sam. 18:7). The Bible presents David as a powerful military leader and a great military strategist. While on the run from Saul, David wreaked havoc on the Philistines with a band of men who were a bunch of misfits. But David shaped these misfits into an effective small army. They are described as relatives and other "men who were in trouble or in debt or who were just discontented—until David was the captain of about 400 men" (1 Sam. 22:2). He was also creative—who else would have acted insane, scratching on doors and drooling down his beard to get away from the Philistine King Achish of Gath while running from Saul (see 1 Sam. 21:13)?

We also know and have heard sermons and teachings on David's failure with Bathsheba, and his murder of her husband, Uriah. It's interesting how the rabbis of old have a different way of looking at this. They assert that David was "one of the few pious men over whom the evil inclination had no powers. By nature he was not disposed to commit such evil-doing as his relation to Bathsheba involved." So they have to explain all of what David did so that David is not guilty of what he did—if that makes sense. To do this, they are willing to put the blame on God. They said that "God Himself brought him to his crime, that He might say to other sinners: 'Go to David and learn how to repent.'"[2] They go on to say that David was guilty neither of murder nor of adultery, for "there were extenuating circumstances." But I think that David knew that what he had done was wrong, for when Nathan confronted him, there was no hesitation in his repentance. In fact, as we will see, David condemned himself for what he did. And David's example does teach us how to repent.

What We Often Overlook

If the ancient rabbis tried to preserve David's goodness by ignoring his dark side, we have a tendency to do the same thing. The fact is that David did much more evil than Saul did, yet God continued to honor him as a man after His own heart. Perhaps we get it wrong sometimes. With God, it seems that He's not as bothered as we think He is with our propensity to sin—He knows that about us. We are all sinners, and we will always be sinners. What He is most concerned with has to do with our heart—with what we do about our sinning. And that was where David excelled. The rabbis were right about one thing; David does teach us how to repent.

It's interesting that as long as there was conflict in David's life, or when he was the underdog and running from Saul, his life seemed to be for the most part one of integrity. But when everything started to settle down and he was comfortably enthroned as king—that was when he failed. David was patient after Saul died. He didn't rush in and claim the throne. He waited. Read 2 Samuel 1–4, and watch how David managed to gradually exercise his claim to the throne. Even though he had been chosen to be king by Samuel under the direction and blessing of God, that didn't mean all the people were ready for him. David knew this; so when he heard of Saul and Jonathan's death, he headed to Hebron, which was his base of operation in the territory of Judah, David's tribe. Saul was from the tribe of Benjamin, and his tribe was part of the north, what was called Israel. So David worked to solidify the support of the people of Judah and only then began to wait on God regarding the followers of Saul.

The throne of the king was inherited, so with the death of Saul, there was no king in Israel. There were those who could claim the throne, and the followers of Saul assumed that Saul's surviving oldest son, Ish-bosheth, would be the next king. In fact, he was crowned king in Israel and actually ruled for two years. Abner, Saul's faithful general, helped make that happen out of loyalty to Saul.

All of this, however, was counter to what God wanted and expected. David was God's choice, and David knew that, for Samuel had anointed him king by God's will. But David had to proceed cautiously. And he did. One by one the opposition went away. Abner was killed, as was Ish-bosheth. In these four chapters (2 Sam. 1–4), we can see what a shrewd and powerful leader David was as each of the claimants to the throne was eliminated, and David was innocent of any involvement. As David waited, he "became stronger and stronger, while Saul's dynasty became weaker and weaker" (2 Sam. 3:1).

But there is a dark side to David. When we go back to the time of his running from Saul, David and his men apparently lived by what could be called extortion. If what David requested from Nabal had been a request by the Mafia, we would call it protection money, which is a form of extortion. Here's what happened. David sent word to Nabal during the celebration marking the sheering of Nabal's 3,000 sheep, and said, "While your shepherds stayed among us near Carmel, we never harmed them, and nothing was ever stolen from them. . . . So would you be kind to us, since we have come at a time of celebration? Please share any provisions you might have on hand with us and with your friend David" (1 Sam. 25:7-8).

Perhaps you may think this sounds like a simple request—not some extortion demanded for protecting Nabal's property. But David's response made it clear that it was extortion. Something was expected of Nabal; for when Nabal refused the request, David and his men were prepared to kill Nabal and take what they had asked for. Only the quick thinking of Nabal's wife Abigail, kept David from killing Nabal. When Nabal died soon after, it freed Abigail to marry David.

Perhaps the most devastating thing that David allowed to happen while running was in his encounter with the priest Ahimelech. He asked Ahimelech for food and was given the only food the priest had, the Bread of the Presence. This was a holy bread that was reserved only for the priests. But out of loyalty, Ahimelech gave it to David. Then David asked for a weapon and was given Goliath's sword. There was no problem in what he was asking, especially since he told Ahimelech that he was on a mission for the king—a half-truth. But then David saw Doeg, Saul's chief herdsman, observing all this, and David did nothing about Doeg. He had to know that Doeg would report what he had seen to Saul, and that Saul, in his paranoia, would take revenge on the priest. But he had no idea the extent of that revenge.

Doeg did tell Saul about what had happened, and Saul sent for
Ahimelech and all his family. Ahimelech tried to tell Saul what he
had done and why, but Saul never heard any of his explanation or
defense. In his rage, Saul ordered his men to kill Ahimelech and all
his family. Saul's request was so outrageous that his men refused to
carry out the order. So Saul turned to Doeg and said, "You do it"
and he did. That day, 85 priests were slaughtered by Doeg, each
"still wearing their priestly garments. Then he went to Nob, the
town of the priests, and killed the priests' families—men and women,
children and babies—and all the cattle, donkeys, sheep, and goats"
(1 Sam. 22:18-19). One man escaped and fled to David, reporting to
him all that had just happened. And David said, "I knew it!" And he
took full responsibility for what had happened. Even in his failures,
David had the capacity to confront and acknowledge his mistakes.
Although the mistake was due to David's failure, his owning his
mistake was part of his strength of character. His attitude is a lesson for each of us, for we need to see our own mistakes in concrete
ways, as David did.

When we come to 2 Samuel 11, we see David at his worst. This
chapter is about his affair with Bathsheba, and this becomes the pivotal turning point in David's life. After this, he will never again be the
man he was. Walter Brueggemann points out that the inspired writer
of this event cuts "very, very deep into the strange web of foolishness,
fear, and fidelity that comprises the human map. This narrative is
more than we want to know about David and more than we can bear
to understand about ourselves."[3] We know the story, but we often
wish that we had never been told the story, or better yet, that it had
never happened. If only David could rewind the video of his life, just
as we often wish we could undo the damage we have caused. Again,
we are grateful that God didn't whitewash the account of David's life,
for we would have missed so much of ourselves that we can see in
him. Brueggemann says that David's sin here "cuts so sharply that it
rivals in power the 'original' act of Adam and Eve."[4] I don't think he
exaggerates. Let's look at what is often overlooked.

David stayed home rather than be present at the front of his army
to lead them. The writer of the text sets it up for us so beautifully—

"In the spring of the year, when kings normally go out to war. . . . David stayed behind in Jerusalem" (2 Sam. 11:1). Why did he stay behind? There are several reasons why he might have stayed home. One is that he simply was exhausted, and since the Ammonites were already defeated, he really wasn't needed. Or perhaps he was told to stay home in order to protect his life—no need to risk the life of the king in a battle that was basically won. This is also what happens in the later battle against Absalom—David is not part of the fighting force. But perhaps it was simply the fact that David was bored—the challenges were over and now what was left was to stabilize the gains. Not much of a challenge for a dynamic leader like David. Regardless of the reason, his staying home left David open to temptation that he chose not to resist.

The unthinkable happens—a one-night stand and it's over, so he thinks. But it wasn't over, for the lady became pregnant. Easy solution—get the husband to come home and sleep with his wife. But Uriah had too strong a sense of loyalty—he wouldn't sleep with his wife while the other troops were in battle. So there was no option left for David except to eliminate Uriah, and that's the course he took. Even though he murdered one of his loyal men by having him put on the front line of the battle, when it was all done, David breathed a sigh of relief and married Bathsheba. No one would ever need to know the truth. But it was not all done, for David forgot that the Lord knew what had occurred—every bit of what had occurred. The text simply says that "the LORD was displeased with what David had done. So the LORD sent Nathan the prophet to tell David this story" (2 Sam. 11:27–12:1).

Now, to confront the king was no small matter, for others had brought reports to David that he didn't like, and they died for their efforts. But Nathan was the prophet, and he was obedient to God's instructions. He told David a story about a rich man who coveted a poor man's one and only little lamb, even though the rich man had many lambs of his own. That little lamb was all the poor man had and was like the family pet. However, when guests arrived at the rich man's house, the rich man didn't want to slaughter one of his own sheep, so he took the poor man's little lamb and killed it and fed it to his guests. Nathan stops—he has told the story. He waits.

When David heard the story, he was furious! He said the rich man deserved to die, and must repay the poor man four times for what he had taken! Picture the scene. David had responded, and then there was silence. Finally, "Nathan said to David, 'You are that man!'" (2 Sam. 12:7). Nathan went on to tell David all that he had done with Bathsheba and Uriah—nothing was secret to Nathan. Then Nathan said David wouldn't die, but there would be a fourfold punishment for his acts, and that one of the consequences would be that what David had done in secret with Bathsheba, someone else would do in public with David's wives. When David hears this, he confesses to Nathan, "I have sinned against the LORD" (2 Sam. 12:13).

Let's look at the fourfold consequences that David imposed on himself in his response to Nathan's story. First, Nathan told David he wouldn't die, but he said that the first consequence was that the baby born of the adulterous act would die. Very soon, the child took sick. David fasted and prayed for seven days, desperately trying to change God's mind, but the prophecy of Nathan came true and the child died. Immediately, David stopped his fast and then comforted Bathsheba. They slept together and she conceived again, and this time the child was born and lived. He was named Solomon.

Then, in the next chapter of 2 Samuel, the second consequence takes place. We will see that the next three consequences of David's sin are also a consequence of David's failure as a father. One of David's sons—the second in line as an heir to the throne, was Absalom. He had a beautiful sister named Tamar. The prince who was first in line as an heir to the throne was Amnon, and he fell in love with his half-sister Tamar. He was so in love with her that he was what you could call lovesick. And because Tamar was a virgin, he felt it was hopeless for him to ever be with her. But Amnon had a crafty cousin who came up with a plan for Amnon to be with Tamar. Amnon was to pretend to be sick and ask that Tamar would prepare some food for him. When she came to his place, she prepared food, but Amnon wouldn't eat it, at first. Then he asked that she feed him while he was in bed. He dismissed all the servants, and when alone with Tamar, over her desperate objections, he raped her. As soon as he completed the horrible act, his love turned to hate, and he sent her away.

Tamar was ruined! She tore off the robe of her virginity and put ashes on her head as she left Amnon. Absalom met her as she left, after she had torn off the robe. He knew instantly what had happened to her, and he comforted his sister. He told her not to worry, implying that he would take care of it. "When King David heard what had happened, he was very angry" (2 Sam. 13:21). But he did nothing! Did he know this was one of the consequences of his own adultery? We don't know, but regardless of his own issues, this was something that required a father's hand. Amnon must be dealt with and Tamar must be comforted. But David did nothing.

Two years passed. Tamar lived as a desolate woman in her brother Absalom's house. Now that she was no longer a virgin, no one would marry her, even if she was the king's daughter. Two years of silence. David said and did nothing. Absalom said nothing and did nothing. But he was patiently plotting revenge. Finally, Absalom planned a party during the celebratory time of the sheering of his sheep. He wanted his father to come, but he knew that David wouldn't come. So after begging his father to come, he then asked that Amnon be allowed to come. He pressed David until David agreed. When the party began, the wine flowed freely. Eventually, Amnon got drunk, and at a given signal, Absalom's men rose up and murdered Amnon. Tamar had been avenged! The third consequence had taken place. David's son, the crown prince Amnon, was dead.

At first, the messengers came and told David that Absalom had killed all of his sons. But soon after, cousin Jonadab arrived to say that only Amnon was dead. The text tells us that David mourned many days for his son Amnon. But again he did nothing. Absalom, on the other hand, fled to his grandfather. He stayed there in self-imposed exile for three years. We read, "King David, now reconciled to Amnon's death, longed to be reunited with his son Absalom" (2 Sam. 13:39). The solution to their separation was in David's hand; after all, he was the king. But again, all through those three years, David did nothing.

Finally, David's general, Joab, decided to do something about the estrangement between David and Absalom. Again, a story was used to get David's attention. Joab got a woman from Tekoa to ask David for help. She told David that one of her sons had killed her other son, and that her family demanded justice. She said she was a widow and needed David's help in protecting her remaining son. When David agreed and gave her several reassurances of his protection, she asked for one more thing—"Why don't you do as much for the people of God as you have promised to do for me?" (2 Sam. 14:13). She confronted David about doing the same for Absalom.

David could smell the hand of Joab in this, and he asked the woman if Joab had put her up to this. She admitted it, and David called for Joab to "bring back the young man Absalom" (v. 21). Now, for some strange reason, after Joab had gone after Absalom, David added a strange twist to his order. He said that "Absalom may go to his own house, but he must never come into my presence" (v. 24). What an absurd condition! David longed for his son, but then decreed that his son could never come into his presence. Again, we have the "do-nothing" father. But without David's knowing it, he was setting the stage for the fourth consequence—the rebellion and death of his son Absalom.

Absalom put up with this arrangement for two years and then he got tired of it. He wanted to see his father. He tried and tried to contact the go-between, Joab, but Joab ignored him. Finally Absalom set fire to one of Joab's fields, and that got a response from Joab. Absalom asked Joab why his father had brought him back to Jerusalem if he had no intention of seeing him. He added that he would rather his father kill him than continue this charade. Finally, Joab convinces David, and Absalom is invited by David to come into his presence. When he did, Absalom bowed before his father, and his father kissed him—that's all we are told.

For the next four years, Absalom became the consummate politician. He got up early every morning and would meet the people at the city gate. He would judge cases for the people and give the people justice. He acted toward the people with great humility, never allowing anyone to bow before him. At the four-year mark, he asked his father for permission to go and worship in Hebron, the seat of David's power. But he didn't go just to worship— he went to start a rebellion, a coup d'état! Several of David's inner circle of advisors joined up with Absalom against David.

When David found out, he was told that "all Israel has joined Absalom in a conspiracy against you!" (2 Sam. 15:13). So David set about to get out of Jerusalem and to prepare for battle against his son. Before the battle, Absalom returned to Jerusalem in a mark of triumph. He was told by his advisor to go and sleep with David's concubines, so he set up a tent on the roof of the palace and "had sex with his father's concubines" (2 Sam. 16:22) in full view of the people of Jerusalem. It was an act of conquest, not of the concubines, but of his father, David. It was also a direct fulfillment of what the prophet Nathan had foretold.

When the battle finally commenced, David was told to stay away. He agreed, and his only request was, "For my sake, deal gently with young Absalom" (2 Sam. 18:5). The battle went well and David's forces won a decisive victory. But then the strangest thing happened—as Absalom was riding his horse, he was caught in a tree by his hair and was left swinging helplessly between heaven and earth. One of the men who had heard David's request to deal gently with Absalom found him, and not knowing what to do, came and told Joab. He had followed the king's request, but Joab didn't. Joab made sure that Absalom died in the battle—the fourth consequence!

When David was told about the fate of his son, he was overcome with emotion. He wept as he cried, "O my son Absalom! My son, my son Absalom! If only I had died instead of you! O Absalom, my son, my son" (v. 33). This is one of the saddest images I find in all of Scripture! If I had been there, I think I would have wanted to grab him by the shoulders and shake him and say, "If you wish you had died instead, then why didn't you talk to him when he was still alive! Why this stupid charade of not talking?"

The sadness of his lament is a challenge to parents to take the initiative in keeping communication open with their children. But David was a failure as a father and, yes, the rebellion and death of Absalom was predicted by Nathan; but David, by his inaction was an accomplice to the outcome. It's tragic that he couldn't act on his love for Absalom when his son was alive.

Sin has its consequences. We can see that in David. But what we also see is the effect that sin had on his character and his confidence. Prior to David's affair with Bathsheba, David was a shrewd and confident leader, both militarily and politically. After the affair, David still could lead his army, but he was not the same David. Joab even had to rebuke him for his weeping and mourning for Absalom. Then we hear very little of the David of old, for he wasn't the man he used to be.

So What Can We Learn

I have always been fascinated by the comparison of David with Saul. Why did David retain the blessing and anointing of the Lord when Saul had God's blessing and anointing removed? In many ways, at least humanly speaking, Saul was a better man than David. The evidence suggests that Saul was a good father. His sons were loyal to him, even to the death. Yes, Jonathan, in his loyalty to David, kept him informed about his father Saul's actions; but in doing this he never acted in a disloyal way to his father. Jonathan was at his father's side in the final battle as they died together. Saul's daughter Michel did Saul's bidding in terms of marriage. She married David, then when David fled Saul, she married another man at her father's direction. None of Saul's children ever rebelled against him.

When it came to his followers, Saul's army never turned against him. Yes, when Samuel was late in coming to make the sacrifice, some were going home, but that wasn't in rebellion to Saul. They were assuming that without a sacrifice God wouldn't be with them in the battle, so there would be no battle. They were not rebelling. But David, for all of his leadership abilities, had some of his most trusted aides turn against him and side with Absalom. And even his own son turned against him.

Saul was obedient to God's command that when Israel got a king, he was to have only one wife (see Deut. 17:17), whereas David had at least eight wives, plus countless concubines. David gave in to the cultural expectations of a king. In this way, David was like all the other kings of his day and time—lots of wives and even more concubines. His son Solomon continued and even expanded on this behavior.

Saul's reign was cut off by God for what appears to be a simple act of disobedience—simple when compared to David's disobedience. Yet God continued to bless David to the very end. What was the difference? I think the difference is found in their reactions to confrontations by the prophet Samuel. When Samuel confronted Saul in 1 Samuel 15, Saul basically said, "Okay, I sinned against you and God. Now can we get on with it and offer the sacrifice together so I won't be embarrassed in front of the people?" He was only concerned with appearances. He was caught up in what he assumed was his own power and image. When David was confronted by Nathan in 2 Samuel 12, his immediate response was, "I have sinned against the Lord!" Not "I have sinned against Bathsheba, or against Uriah, or against you, Nathan." No, he knew he had sinned against the Lord! And he offered no excuse and did not care how he looked to those watching the exchange between him and Nathan. He didn't point out that Uriah was an outsider. He simply admitted his sin. The rabbis were correct—David knew how to repent. And he expanded later on his act of repentance in front of Nathan with his psalm of repentance:

> Have mercy on me, O God, because of your unfailing love. Because of your great compassion, blot out the stain of my sins. Wash me clean from my guilt. Purify me from my sin. For I recognize my rebellion; it haunts me day and night. Against you, and you alone, have I sinned; I have done what is evil in your sight (Ps. 51:1-4).

David sinned, as we all do, but as compared to Saul, David knew how to get his heart back in tune with God's heart. That's why God could say that David was a man after His own heart. Their hearts connected. In God's economy, it's not the sinning as much as it is the repenting. And the heart that knows how to repent is a heart after God's own heart.

There is a second thing we can learn from David. In his lament over the death of Saul and Jonathan, David said:

> Oh, how the mighty heroes have fallen in battle! Jonathan lies dead on the hills. How I weep for you, my brother Jonathan! Oh, how much I loved you! And your love for me was deep, deeper than the love of women! Oh, how the mighty heroes have fallen! Stripped of their weapons, they lie dead (2 Sam. 1:25-27).

For one thing, David knew how to grieve. He led the people of Israel in grieving over Saul and Jonathan. But in the midst of his grief, he made a statement that often makes men uncomfortable. He said that the love of Jonathan was deeper than the love of women. What David discovered was that for a man, the strength of his character is built on his ability to relate deeply to the other men in his life. Unfortunately, many men today don't know how to have deep friendships with other men. They don't even have another man they can rely on or be accountable to. Oh, they can talk sports, or the stock market or cars; but to talk about heart matters—that's not masculine. As a result, when a man struggles, he typically struggles alone. He has no male friends on whom he can depend.

We have men calling us on the *New Life* radio program, and they are in crisis. Invariably when we ask a man if he has any male friends, his answer is no. The guy's wife has left him, and he has no other man he can lean on. Our advice is always the same—you need to get into a small group of men who will be committed to each other. We need male "covenant" relationships. To do this, we need to get over our fear of loving another man.

For David, the depth of his friendship with Jonathan was a key to their success as men. There was no "going it alone" for either of them. They weren't together much in the later years before Jonathan died, but they were in a "covenant" relationship, and it was a source of their strength of character. It is a lesson every man needs to learn—to understand the difference between the love and commitment of male relationships, and the love of a woman. Men today are more comfortable talking about the love of a woman, but we need to become comfortable with the healthy love relationships we must have with other men. I'm fortunate in that I have five men I can count on to stand by me—one of them my dearest friend I've known since I was a freshman in college.

Third, and perhaps the most important lesson we can learn from David is in his relationship with God. We said earlier that God doesn't seem to be as concerned about our sinning as He is about the condition of our heart relationship with Him. This is seen clearly when we compare Saul and David. Saul was more concerned with his image than he was with his heart relationship with God. That wasn't so with David. Throughout his life, in most situations, David was concerned with what God wanted in the situation. That sensitivity gave him a soft heart in his relationship with God—a heart that God could access. We need to guard our hearts. We need to keep from developing the hardness of heart that will separate us not only from those we love but from God Himself. We need a heart like David's—the kind of heart that knows how to repent. May we each have such a heart!

#

SOME SAINTLY WOMEN

*"Look," Naomi said to her, "your sister-in-law has gone back to her
people and to her gods. You should do the same." But Ruth replied,
"Don't ask me to leave you and turn back. Wherever you go, I will go;
wherever you live, I will live. Your people will be my people,
and your God will be my God."*

RUTH 1:15-16

*Barak told her, "I will go, but only if you go with me."
"Very well," she replied. "I will go with you. But you will receive
no honor in this venture, for the LORD's victory over Sisera will be
at the hands of a woman."*

JUDGES 4:8-9

*Mordecai sent this reply to Esther: "Don't think for a moment that
because you're in the palace you will escape when all other Jews are killed.
If you keep quiet at a time life this, deliverance and relief will arise from some
other place. . . . Who knows if perhaps you were made queen
for just such a time as this?*

ESTHER 4:13-14

The Swiss psychiatrist Paul Tournier raises an important question in his little book *To Resist or to Surrender?* He begins with the story of a young German theologian named Dr. Eberhard Muller, who at the beginning of World War II was serving as a chaplain in

Russia. He clearly saw what was coming with the rise of the Nazis and the Third Reich, and he believed that his country was being "poisoned by the Nazi ideology. It had penetrated into all the areas of professional and social life, especially among the younger people. Teachers had to inculcate it; jurists and physicians had to apply its laws, directly destroying the dignity of men."[1] Muller then asked the question as to who would straighten everything out. Who would resist the Nazi ideology, and who would surrender to it. His answer was "the church, of course."

But history has shown that many in the leadership of the churches of Germany surrendered their values and simply became part of the Nazi regime. That wasn't true of everyone, for there were also parts of the Church who did not surrender, but resisted and stood firm in their beliefs and values in spite of the Nazi regime. Many of them paid the ultimate price for their resistance, as they chose to risk death rather than surrender.

We fight the same battle today. As believers, do we simply join with the culture, or do we resist its secular and materialistic pressures? Many believe that today parts of our American faith community have surrendered to the pressures of the culture. Too many churches today judge themselves by corporate standards like "How big are we?" or "How exciting is our product—our programs?" or "How popular is our CEO—our senior pastor?" While this is often seen in the Western world, in other parts of the world Christians don't ask these questions. They are too busy surviving persecution, as they resist their culture and in simple ways seek to build a body of believers; doing this in the face of persecution, prison and even death.

Individually we all face this choice at various points in our life—do we resist and stand firm, or do we slide into surrender, where we simply give in to the pressures of our culture? Three women stand out in the Old Testament, who when faced with this question, stood firm and followed God despite a culture that would have never noticed if they had simply surrendered and quietly gone along.

Not many women are highlighted in the Old Testament. To understand this we must remember that they lived in a patriarchal culture, where the men were the dominant figures. If a woman is highlighted in the Old Testament, she stands above the men of her time. Prior to this, in the discussion of the men of the Old Testament, we have also looked at Sarah, Rebekah, Leah and Rachel, and Moses' sister Miriam as great women of faith. But each of these women lived in the shadow of a dominant male figure. When we come to Naomi and Ruth, or Deborah or Esther, we are in the presence of women saints who stood tall because they did not surrender to the ways of the culture, choosing instead to resist the culture and do the right thing.

Ruth and Naomi

According to the ancient rabbis, the story of Ruth and Naomi takes place about 100 years after the time of Israel's first judge, Othniel, and before the time of the woman judge, Deborah. Historically, Ruth comes first in our trilogy. Following the death of Othniel, the "LORD gave King Eglon of Moab control over Israel because of their evil" (Judg. 3:12). From the death of Othniel until the next judge, Ehud, the Israelites were dominated by the Moabites. So it makes sense that when famine hit the land of Israel, many of the Israelites went to live in the country of Moab. Naomi and her husband Elimelech, along with their two sons, were part of that migration. Once there, they settled in the land of Moab. After some time, Elimelech died, leaving Naomi to survive with her two sons. Eventually, each of Naomi's two sons married a local woman, a woman of Moab. One son "married a woman named Orpah, and the other a woman named Ruth" (Ruth 1:4).

As the ancient rabbis tell the story, those who lived in Moab were told that the men from Israel could marry a local Moabite woman, but that the Israelite women were not allowed to marry Moabite men. This will play out later in the rabbis' version of the story of Ruth. Then, 10 years after Elimelech dies, the unthinkable happens to Naomi; her two sons die. Since they were her only source of livelihood, and since she couldn't marry a Moabite man, she determined to return to Bethlehem and to her extended family. Her two daughters-in-law accompanied her at first, but then

Naomi realized that just as there was no future for her in Moab, there would be no future for either Orpah or Naomi in Israel. In fact, not being Jewish would mean they would probably be persecuted, and life would be extremely difficult for them.

Orpah decides to return to her family in Moab, but Ruth makes that profound profession of loyalty to her mother-in-law, quoted at the beginning of the chapter. She added, "May the LORD punish me severely if I allow anything but death to separate us!" (Ruth 1:17). So Naomi said nothing more, and Ruth stayed with her as they returned to Bethlehem. During this time, Naomi probably instructed Ruth in the customs of the Jews and how she was to behave in Israel.

Naomi also had a plan. She knew that Boaz was related to her late husband and could be what was called the "family redeemer." In the Jewish culture, the family redeemer had three main responsibilities. First, if a member of the family became so poor that he lost his land, the family redeemer was to purchase the land so it would remain in the family. Second, if a member of the family became so poor that he had to sell himself into slavery, the family redeemer would pay off his debt, and then the person would pay back the family redeemer by working for the family, not for the debt holder. Third, if an Israelite was killed by someone outside the family, the family redeemer was to pursue justice for the one killed. The role of the family redeemer would fall on the oldest and closest relative. (For more detail on the family redeemer, see Leviticus 25:23-55 and Numbers 35:16-21. The role of family redeemer is acted out in Ruth 4.)

But Boaz wasn't the closest relative to Naomi's deceased husband, since he had an older brother, Tob. That's the name given to the man by the rabbis. In the account given in the book of Ruth, there are just too many complications for Tob to redeem Naomi's land and marry Ruth—all part of the family redeemer's responsibility. What the rabbis added was that Tob thought the injunction against marrying a Moabite was that no one could marry a Moabite—neither male nor female. He didn't know that the injunction only applied to an Israelite woman marrying a Moabite man (which Boaz understood). So Tob told Boaz he was free to do the acts of redeeming—because he himself just couldn't do it.

What began as an impossible circumstance for both Ruth and Naomi ended with Boaz marrying Ruth, and eventually a son was born of their union. It was a boy named Obed, who became the father of Jesse, who became the father of King David. And that's how the book of Ruth ends. A very sad beginning with a very happy ending. But as we'll see, there's always more.

Deborah

Not long after the story of Ruth, we meet another incredible woman named Deborah. She became Israel's only woman judge. The second judge to emerge described in the book of Judges was named Ehud. He killed the Moabite king named Eglon, and then mobilized the Israelites to attack and defeat the Moabite army. This victory led to peace in the land for 80 years. It seemed that as long as a judge lived, Israel behaved in a way that pleased the Lord. But when the judge died, the people returned to their sinful ways, worshipping the pagan gods, not Yahweh their Lord.

Sometime during the 80 years of peace, there was a skirmish with the Philistines in which Shamgar rescued Israel, but he was never listed in the names of the judges. So the next judge to rescue Israel was to be a woman named Deborah.

Frederick Buechner describes Deborah, Israel's only woman judge, as looking "like Golda Meir and doing business under a palm tree. Her business consisted of more than just stepping in and settling things when people got in a wrangle. . . . Whenever there was any fighting to be done, she was the one who was in charge. Even generals jumped when she snapped her fingers."[2] Sounds like a very apt description of this amazing woman.

The pattern was that God would punish the people when they turned away from Him, and He did this through pagan kings. After the judges Ehud and Shamgar fulfilled their tasks by eliminating the oppressive king of their generation, they died. When they left the scene, the next oppressor was King Jabin of Hazor, a

Canaanite king. The commander of this king's army was named Sisera. The ancient rabbis describe him as "really bad" and as "one of the greatest heroes known to history. They said that when he was thirty years old, he had conquered the whole world. At the sound of his voice the strongest of walls fell in a heap, and the wild animals in the woods were chained to the spot by fear."[3] Sounds like an exaggeration to us today, but that was obviously the way Israel experienced the feared Sisera. The text tells us he had 900 iron chariots, which made him an invincible enemy. Obviously, the rabbis gave us a picture of a powerful and ruthless enemy.

When the people had had enough of being persecuted by Sisera and his king, they once again returned to the Lord. And this time, Deborah came to the forefront to rescue Israel. Deborah was both a prophetess and a judge. She would sit under the palm tree and judge the people's issues. She was a forerunner of the role Samuel would play years later—judge, prophet and military leader.

It's interesting that the text says Lappidoth was Deborah's husband, but the rabbis made Barak her husband. It doesn't change the story whether Barak was another name for Lappidoth, or whether they were two different men—either way she called for Barak and told him to gather together 10,000 of his best warriors to face the feared Sisera. In her call, she also said that the Lord would give the Israelites victory over Sisera. Barak was willing, but only if Deborah went with him. Deborah told him she would, but that the honor of the "LORD's victory over Sisera will be at the hands of a woman" (Judg. 4:9). First impression would be that Deborah was to be that woman.

Barak pulled together the army and headed to the Kishon River. Sisera had heard what was happening and had already mobilized his men and his 900 iron chariots and was on his way to the Kishon River as well. But when Barak led his army against Sisera and attacked, the text says "the LORD threw Sisera and all his chariots and warriors into a panic" (Judg. 4:15). Sisera—the fearsome warrior—fell off his chariot and ran away from the battle on foot. At the same time, Barak chased Sisera's army until every one of his warriors had been killed.

Then came the unexpected. Sisera thought he had gotten away, and he ran up to what must have been a familiar tent, for it says that Heber the Kenite—the owner of the tent—was on friendly terms with Sisera's king. Heber, the husband, was ultimately on the side of Israel. He wasn't in the tent—he was in the battle with Barak. But Jael, his wife, was there, and she "seduced" Sisera into the tent. In that day, a woman alone never invited a man into her tent unless she was going to have sex with him. But Jael had a different plan. Sisera asked for water, but Jael went further by not giving him water, she gave him yogurt. Sisera wasn't thinking sex—he was thinking survival, so he instructed Jael to guard the door and if anyone came by and asked, she was to say that no one was inside. Jael did what he asked, but she was really waiting for Sisera to fall asleep.

The rabbis describe the scene this way. They say that Jael had been praying that God would give her a sign to confirm that she was doing God's will. The first sign she asked for was that Sisera would fall asleep. When that happened, she prayed again, this time asking that she would be able to pull Sisera to the floor of the tent without him waking up. And she was able to accomplish that task. Then she took a tent peg and hammered it "through his temple and into the ground, and so he died" (Judg. 4:21).

When Barak arrived at the tent, looking for Sisera, Jael showed Barak the dead Sisera. Based on Deborah's song of victory in which she describes Sisera's mother waiting for him to return home in victory, the rabbis insist that Barak instead sent Sisera's dead body back to his mother. That was the beginning of Israel's throwing off the oppressive King Jabin of Hazor. We are told that as long as Deborah lived—which was 40 years—peace was in the land of Israel. But the woman who received the honor for the defeat of Sisera wasn't Deborah, it was Jael.

Esther

The story of Esther takes place more than 600 years after Deborah, and was probably the last book of the Old Testament to be written. The story takes place during the reign of the Persian King

Xerxes, who reigned between 486 and 465 BC, and begins during the third year of Xerxes's reign, which would be about 483 BC. The story comes to a peak between 474 and 473 BC—during the twelfth year of the reign of King Xerxes.

Most are familiar with the details of the story—how Esther became the queen, how Haman hated the Jews and got Xerxes to issue a decree whereby all Jews were to be killed. How Mordecai, Esther's cousin, had saved the king's life; and then there was all the intrigue that took place in the struggle between Mordecai and Haman. Finally, Esther won the day; Haman was executed and Mordecai became the prime minister. The Jewish feast of Purim commemorates the events in Esther, especially the hanging of Haman and the saving of the lives of all the Jews. This festival has taken place faithfully every year for almost 2,500 years.

It's also interesting to note that the book of Esther is the only book in the Bible that doesn't mention the name of God or even refer to God. But when we read the story, it isn't difficult to see God's hand in every event, from the total despair of the Jews who thought they were going to be killed, all the way to the happy ending. But the ancient rabbis add some interesting detail, some of which is probably based on the oral traditions that were passed down from rabbi to rabbi, and from the people of Esther's generation to the next, and then the next beyond that and so on.

According to the rabbis, Esther's mother died as she gave birth to her, and her father had died just prior to her birth. She was adopted by her cousin Mordecai and his wife and accepted as if she was their literal daughter. Mordecai was of the tribe of Benjamin, a descendant of King Saul, and he belonged to the highest aristocracy of Jerusalem.

As the story begins in the book of Esther, Xerxes's rule extended over 127 provinces. He had invited all the rulers of these provinces, who served under him, to a six-month celebration, followed by a week of feasting and drinking—called a banquet, but it really was an extended banquet. On the seventh day of feasting and drinking, Xerxes, who "was in high spirits because of the wine" (Esther 1:10), ordered his queen, Vashti, to come and show all the men how beautiful she was. That's what we read in the Bible, but the rabbis tell us that what Xerxes actually ordered was for her to come and stand naked in front of all the princes. She was ordered to literally show herself. She refused to respond to the order, and Xerxes was left with a problem. If he let Vashti get away with ignoring his order, all the wives in the country would soon be ignoring and disobeying their husbands. So an example had to be made of Vashti. According to the rabbis, she was executed. Then, in order to cover all the bases, a decree went out from Xerxes saying that women must obey their husbands.

Now the king was left without a queen, so an order was given to find a new queen, and Esther would eventually be chosen. But first she had to go through a year long process of preparation. Hegai was the eunuch in charge of the harem, and it was his duty to prepare Esther and all the other contestants. As he worked on preparing the candidates, he favored Esther and was willing to let her eat a diet that was permitted to Jews, instead of the food from the royal table.

When Esther was chosen as queen, it followed that Mordecai would have some position in the king's court. His appointment displaced two chamberlains—Bigthan and Teresh—who were released from their duties. This resulted in their plotting how they would poison the king. Since, according to the rabbis, Mordecai was a member of the Sanhedrin, he knew "all the seventy languages of the world."[4] So even though Bigthan and Teresh talked together in their own language, Mordecai could understand them. Since he knew about the plot, he revealed it to Xerxes, thus saving the king's life.

This conspiracy led Xerxes to never have two chamberlains protect him—only one, and the new one appointed was Haman. Xerxes was thinking that he was wise in doing this—to play Haman against Mordecai. Xerxes believed that if he had honored Mordecai for saving his life, Mordecai would ask for permission to rebuild the Temple in Jerusalem. Xerxes did not want that to happen, for he believed that would empower the Jews. So he simply didn't reward Mordecai.

An interesting sidelight shared by the rabbis is the story behind the hatred of Haman toward the Jews, and especially toward
Mordecai. It seems that a city in India rebelled against Xerxes, and
troops were dispatched under the command of Haman and Mordecai. Provisions were given to last three years, the estimated time
for the campaign. By the end of the first year, Haman had squan-
dered all of his provisions, and he asked Mordecai for some of his.
Mordecai refused, for it would have impacted the men under his
command. Haman begged in a variety of ways, and each time
Mordecai refused. Finally, out of desperation, Haman offered to
become Mordecai's slave, and Mordecai agreed, writing the "bill
of sale" on Mordecai's kneecap. Some years later, when Haman
was honored by the king, every time Mordecai would see him he
would stretch out his knee toward Haman as a reminder.

The other thing the rabbis add to the story is that when
Haman made everyone bow to him in his presence, Mordecai
wouldn't do it. The reason he wouldn't bow was that Haman had
intentionally tied an idol to his belt. If Mordecai had bowed to
Haman, he would also have been bowing to a pagan idol. Mordecai would rather die first than bow to any man, but even more so,
to bow to an idol.

Esther's marriage to the pagan Xerxes was a sore point with
the rabbis. Their defense of this was that Esther's "marriage with
Ahasuerus (Xerxes) was but a feigned union. God had sent down
a female spirit in the guise of Esther to take her place with the
king. Esther herself never lived with Ahasuerus as his wife."[5] What
bothered them doesn't seem to be an issue to us anymore, especially when we see how God put Esther there, for in the words of
Mordecai, "Who knows if perhaps you were made queen for just
such a time as this?" (Esther 4:14). And the lesson to us is who
knows what God has in store for us, even in the midst of terrible
circumstances.

All through the ancient rabbis' account of Esther was the description of God's activity in all that went on. God prepared the
way for Esther to be queen. God protected her when she went in
uninvited before the king. God protected Mordecai against Ha-

man. God caused Xerxes to be unable to sleep so that he could be reminded that Mordecai had never been honored. How else could that have been so timely unless God was behind it all? And it was God who gave Esther the words to say to the king on each occasion. And it was God who turned what appeared to be a holocaust of gigantic proportions to a victory for the Jews and a happy ending that included a festive (Purim) celebration that continues to this day.

So What Can We Learn?

What are some of the common threads that run through the stories of these three incredible women? The first thing is that each of them couldn't have done it alone; they needed someone they could trust alongside them. Ruth needed Naomi to teach her the customs of the Jews; Deborah needed Barak to lead the army into battle; and Esther wouldn't have known what was going on in the realm if it wasn't for Mordecai and his challenge to her.

This has been a pattern with most everyone we've looked at after Genesis, beginning with Moses. Moses had his brother Aaron and his sister Miriam; Saul had Samuel, even though he didn't really listen to Samuel. David had Nathan, who was able to confront him about his sin; and we'll see that Elijah had Elisha. The development of our faith is not something we do on our own. It is done in a community we call "church." When we try to go it alone, we don't get very far, and we are vulnerable to the wiles and temptations of the enemy of our soul. Our blind spots distort our vision of ourselves, resulting in our falsely thinking that we have it all together. But when we bring our faith-walk into relationship, we are able to see where we are failing, or where we still need to grow.

The second thing we can learn from these three women is how we are to view our circumstances—especially the circumstances we wish would go away. Each of these stories began in what appeared to be a hopeless situation. What chance did the Moabite Ruth have to assimilate into the Jewish culture of Bethlehem, let alone find a husband? It was so impossible that it wasn't even on Ruth and Naomi's radar at first—all they could think about was getting enough to eat just to survive. But they were open and God made a way for them that took them way beyond just surviving.

The people of Israel lived in fear of Sisera, the powerful general of King Jabin of Hazor. Jabin and Sisera had made life miserable for Israel. All appeared to be hopeless. They were destined to be subject to the whims of Jabin, and especially Sisera. Yet, in the midst of despair, a woman named Deborah heard from the Lord and called for a battle, and the impossible took place—Israel defeated Sisera.

And how was Esther to do anything? The Jewish people felt hopeless. On an appointed day in March, they were all to be exterminated. Esther, even though she was queen, had no power and hadn't even been in the presence of King Xerxes for a month. How was she to intercede, especially since she would risk death if she came before him uninvited? And then there was the fact that once a decree went out from Xerxes, it couldn't be changed. To all involved, it was an impossible situation.

Three hopeless situations if viewed from a human perspective. Yet each situation had a happy ending. Why? Because in each of these situations, these women interpreted their circumstances in the light of who God was (and is). They didn't define God by the circumstances.

I talk with many people who define God according to their circumstances. They say "God isn't really God, for He hasn't provided the job I desperately need," or "the healing from cancer I need," or "the money I need just to pay my bills and eat. I'm ready to give up on God because I'm in a tough situation and He hasn't rescued me." They look at something Paul wrote to the Corinthians that says, "God is faithful, He will not allow the temptation to be more than you can stand" (1 Cor. 10:13). They say, "This is way more than I can stand—so where is God?" They are defining God through their circumstances. The circumstances are frustratingly painful, and they believe that God has let them down. In spite of what any of us are experiencing, Paul begins that promise with the affirmation that "God is faithful." We can't let any circumstance negate that truth!

If we interpret the circumstances based on the character of God, like Ruth, Deborah and Esther did, we will not only endure, but we may also even overcome, and we will certainly grow in our faith and trust of a faithful God. I remember when early in our marriage my wife and I struggled with even getting a paycheck. We were working for an independent youth ministry, and our income was dependent on people's gifts to the ministry. We had bills that were due, and there was no money for us to be paid. It was frustrating. Where was God in all of this? In our struggles, we often redefined God based on our circumstances. But if our circumstances defined God, then He was not being very faithful. But if our understanding of God defined our circumstances, then He was faithful. There was always something God wanted us to learn each time we found ourselves in that situation. We had to learn to depend on God's faithfulness and promise of provision. That was some years ago. We know He was faithful then and He has been faithful all along the way.

In each of these circumstances, God was looking for a willing heart. Not only was Ruth willing to follow Naomi, but she was also immovable in her commitment and resolve to stay with her. Deborah heard the word from God, and she responded to the impossible—defeat Sisera! And Esther was willing even to marry a pagan king, knowing that somewhere in all of it, God was already at work. When told of Xerxes's decree, and when Mordecai told her she had to do something about it, she told Mordecai that she would "go in to see the king. If I must die, I must die" (Esther 4:16). Now that was a willing heart!

Who knows what God has in store for each of us when we learn the lessons taught by the choices of these three incredible women when we have a willing heart to make similar choices.

13

Some Saints Who Were

*Then the woman told Elijah, "Now I know for sure that you are
a man of God, and that the LORD truly speaks through you."*
1 KINGS 17:24

*Go and love your wife again, even though she commits adultery with
another lover. This will illustrate that the LORD still loves Israel, even though
the people have turned to other gods and love to worship them.*
HOSEA 3:1

*Then God said to Jonah, "Is it right for you to be angry because the
plant died?" "Yes," Jonah retorted, "even angry enough to die!"*
JONAH 4:9

*I cry out, "My splendor is gone! Everything I had hoped for
from the LORD is lost!"*
LAMENTATIONS 3:18

I just received the monthly newsletter from my friend Roy Thompson, who is living and ministering with his wife in Thailand. His wife has set up a place of refuge for young women trapped in the world of child trafficking and child prostitution. He wrote:

Pray I never get used to the stories I hear. Last week we interviewed five young adolescents (ages 14 to 18) from the government home for trafficked and abused children. They were all Thai. None had any place to go—no family that cared, no friends outside the government facility. One so wounded that her sentences were not understandable (physical abuse had left her brain damaged), others with single mothers who sold the oldest daughter in order to feed the younger children. Several are the product of rape. Three were street kids—flower sellers, or children who wash your windshield while you wait at the stoplight, usually managed by an "auntie." One was sold at age ten to the same man "in a car" multiple times. The last time she escaped and ran to a policeman (by God's grace, a policeman who happened to care). All four children were taken from her and she is currently serving a 6-10-year jail term. The pedophile was also caught. He was given an $800 fine, no jail time, told not to do it again and then the mother was made to publicly "forgive" him. My heart cries out, *Where is the justice? Especially for women? When does it stop? How bad does it need to be?*

"Out of men's hearts, come evil thoughts, sexual immorality . . . adultery . . . deceit, lewdness" (Mark 7:21-22, *NIV*). For years—long before we moved here—XXX-rated DVDs were available on many vendors' tables, most in plain view and clearly advertised. About two months ago, child pornography began to be advertised to Western customers on those same tables. Thais and Westerners alike were outraged at the open display. The police were called to investigate. Nothing happened. Articles were written in the paper. Nothing happened. Undercover reporters observed. Nothing happened. Police from other precincts complained. Nothing happened. There is a large enough economic payoff in selling child pornography to foreigners (mostly Westerners) that the vendors simply are paying the local police more protection money. Where is the protection for children? God help us!

What he is describing, unfortunately, is happening in multiple places around the world. But there is also nothing new under the sun, for what my friend was describing must have been similar to what Elijah, Jonah, Hosea and Jeremiah, along with the other prophets, encountered as they sought to call Israel and Judah back to their covenant relationship with God.

Elijah was active as a prophet between 870 and 850 BC, during the reign of Israel's King Ahab and his wife Jezebel. It was under their leadership that the worship of Baal began. Jonah and Hosea prophesied between 760 and 722 BC, both preaching in the Northern Kingdom of Israel right up to when the Assyrians took Israel captive. Jeremiah, known as the weeping prophet, prophesied in the Southern Kingdom of Judah between 627 and 580 BC, where he warned the people of coming doom and then watched as Jerusalem fell to the armies of Babylon. We could look at some of the other prophets, but what is interesting about these four is that we know things about their personal lives. And their personal lives add a richness to the lessons they taught during their lifetime, as well as what they can teach us. We'll look at them in chronological order.

Elijah (1 Kings 17–19; 2 Kings 1:1–2:18)

Elijah arrived on the scene at a critical time in the life of Israel. Baal worship had taken over the imagination of the Israelites and they had turned away from the worship of the LORD. Ahab, and especially Jezebel, were the force behind this false religion. Baal was a Canaanite fertility and nature god who was believed to basically control the rain and the crops and, therefore, life itself.

When Israel came into the Promised Land, every village had their own deity of Baal. Their idol would be named "Baal-" and after the hyphen would come the name of their city. The brand of "Baal" that Jezebel brought came from the city of Tyre, her home, was named "Baal-Melqart," and his worship included child sacrifices. Jezebel also set up what was called an Asherah pole, with the focus of their worship a Canaanite mother-goddess. Temple prostitution was a part of their worship. In addition, Jezebel wasn't just satisfied with bringing her own religion to Israel, she also tried her best to exterminate the prophets of God, especially Elijah.

When we understand that Ahab and Jezebel had introduced the worship of a "rain god," we can see the significance of Elijah's prediction that there would be a drought—no rain until he said so. In doing this, the contest between Yahweh and Baal had begun. Jehovah God would hold back the rain as a way of showing that he was the living God, and that Baal was just a worthless piece of carved wood.

Elijah appeared on the scene standing in front of King Ahab, and told the king, "As surely as the LORD, the God of Israel, lives—the God I serve—there will be no dew or rain during the next few years until I give the word!" (1 Kings 17:1). That was a direct challenge to the worship of Baal, and would certainly incur the wrath of Jezebel, so God told Elijah to go and hide beside Kerith Brook. There was water there, and God promised he would provide Elijah with food through the ravens.

The ancient rabbis give us Ahab's side of the conversation. They said that Ahab mocked Elijah and said, "Was not Moses greater than Joshua, and did he not say that God would let no rain descend upon the earth, if Israel served and worshipped idols? There is not an idol known to which I do not pay homage, yet we enjoy all that is goodly and desirable. Dost thou believe that if the words of Moses remain unfulfilled, the words of Joshua will come true?"[1] He brags about his worship of idols and then points out that since God hasn't done anything about it, why should he listen to Elijah?

But this time God acted, and for almost three years, there was no rain. Drought hit Israel, and famine followed. Ahab was desperate to find Elijah, but God protected him. During his time in hiding, Elijah learned daily about God's provision for his sustenance—and for his protection. Finally, God told him it was time to go to Ahab and issue the next challenge. When Ahab saw him, he said, "So, is it really you, you troublemaker of Israel?" (1 Kings 18:17). Elijah responded and issued his challenge to Ahab—and to the prophets of Baal:

> "I have made no trouble for Israel," Elijah replied. "You and your family are the troublemakers, for you have refused to obey the commands of the LORD and have worshiped the images of Baal instead. Now summon all Israel to join me at

Mount Carmel, along with the 450 prophets of Baal, and the 400 prophets of Asherah who are supported by Jezebel" (vv. 18-19).

So the contest was set between Baal and the God of Israel. The rabbis said that twin bulls were chosen, so there would be no advantage to either side. They also said that the bull assigned to the prophets of Baal froze in place. It refused to walk to the altar that was erected by the prophets of Baal. The rabbis went on to say that this young bullock didn't want to enrage his Creator by being sacrificed to a false god. Only when Elijah led him to the altar of Baal, reassuring him that he was serving the Lord in what he was doing, did the bull cooperate. Both bulls were sacrificed, but nothing miraculous occurred with the bull offered to Baal.

When Elijah offered up his bull, he poured water over the altar and all around the altar, then he called down fire from heaven to consume the offering. Elijah and the Lord had a great victory in the miracle of the sacrifice. Then they killed all the prophets of Baal and Asherah. And finally, he prayed for rain, and the rain came.

Now the rabbis are amazed that in "spite of all these miracles, the people persisted in their idolatrous ways and thoughts."[2] But what is amazing to me is Elijah's response to this incredible confirmation of the living God. He had just been part of a miraculous victory over the prophets of Baal and Asherah—and over Ahab and Jezebel. But when Jezebel sent him a message saying, "May the gods strike me and even kill me if by this time tomorrow I have not killed you just as you killed them. Elijah was afraid and fled for his life" (1 Kings 19:2-3). Wait! Isn't this the Elijah that God had protected from Ahab and Jezebel for almost three years? Isn't this the Elijah who had just participated in several incredible miracles? What happened to him?

Probably the same thing happens to us when we've been part of a mighty miracle, or an answer to prayer, or after we see God work in a mighty way. We let up. Hopefully, we don't let up to the same degree that Elijah did, for he ended up depressed and alone, wanting to die. When he got the message from Jezebel, he ran.

After running for who knows how long, in his exhaustion he collapsed under a broom tree. He prayed, "I have had enough, LORD. . . . Take my life, for I am no better than my ancestors who have already died" (v. 4). Yes, he had been part of the defeat of Baal, but Israel hadn't been impressed, or changed—at least in Elijah's eyes—by what had happened. So he felt he was a failure and just wanted to die.

But Elijah didn't die. At the end of his life, he was simply carried away by a whirlwind into heaven in a chariot of fire. Because he didn't die, the rabbis have pages of stories about all the things they believe he had done over the ages to help people. One of the stories is about Rabbi Joshua ben Levi, who wanted to follow Elijah around on his wanderings throughout the world. Elijah said yes, he could follow him, but he couldn't question anything Elijah did. The first night they reached the home of a poor man whose only possession was a cow. Their host couple treated them well, providing food and a place to sleep. But upon leaving, Elijah prayed that their cow would die. Rabbi Joshua was bothered by this, but because of his promise, he couldn't ask any questions. On the next night, a wealthy man let them stay, but didn't offer them any food or drink. This man had a wall that had collapsed and needed repair. But the next morning, as they left, Elijah prayed that the wall would erect itself, and it did. The following night they stayed in a very beautiful synagogue, but the people were cold and inhospitable. When they left the next morning, Elijah prayed that they would all be "heads." Rabbi Joshua was totally confused by all of this.

Finally, Rabbi Joshua had to ask Elijah why he had prayed in such a way. He answered that in the first situation the man's wife was ordained by God to die on the day they left their home. Elijah said he prayed that the death of the cow would substitute for her death in God's eyes. The wall that erected itself had hidden a lot of gold, and if the rich man had rebuilt the wall, he would have found the gold. But when the wall erected itself, the gold remained hidden. And his prayer for all the people in the synagogue to be "heads" meant that Elijah was praying that a "place of numerous leaders is bound to be ruined by reason of the multiplicity of counsel and disputes."[3] With everyone trying to be the leader, chaos would result.

These are fun stories that have a twist, but in the mind of the rabbis, Elijah was and still is alive and active in the world. This is not so far-fetched, really, for in Matthew 17, when Jesus was transfigured on a high mountain in the presence of Peter, James and John, Matthew tells us that "Suddenly, Moses and Elijah appeared and began talking with Jesus" (v. 3). Peter, who saw all of this, wanted to build three shelters—one for Jesus, one for Moses, and one for Elijah.

Although Moses' death is recorded in Deuteronomy 34:6-7, Elijah did not die and was translated directly to heaven (see 2 Kings 2:11). But both Moses and Elijah were, and still are, alive in heaven. They were also alive on that mountain as they were talking with Jesus. We need to understand what Jesus explicitly taught in Matthew 22:31-32—that Old Testament saints in heaven were not dead and gone but were alive and active. He said, "But now, as to whether there will be a resurrection of the dead—haven't you ever read about this in the Scriptures? Long after Abraham, Isaac, and Jacob had died, God said, 'I am the God of Abraham, the God of Isaac, and the God of Jacob.' So he is the God of the living, not the dead." And He still is!

Hosea (Hosea 1–3)

Our next two prophets were active in the same period of time. They preached during the final days of the Northern Kingdom of Israel, when Israel was defeated and taken captive by the Assyrians. The first three chapters of the book of Hosea give us insight into Hosea's life, while the rest of the book is a record of his prophecies. In the beginning of the book, Hosea is told by God to go and marry a prostitute. He does—he marries Gomer. The purpose for this, in God's eyes, it seems, was that Hosea's life was to be an object lesson that would literally show the people of Israel how God experienced his relationship with them. God looked at the people of Israel and said they lived as if they were prostitutes by worshipping the Canaanite gods. So Hosea was to marry someone who was a prostitute to begin with, not knowing the next phase of the object lesson, when she would return to her life as a prostitute.

Hosea and Gomer had three children. Each of them became another part of the object lesson. He was to name each one of them some strange name that would get the attention of the people. The names they were given also reflected God's experience of his relationship with the people. The firstborn was a son named Jezreel, a reference to King Jehu's murder of the people in the Valley of Jezreel (see 2 Kings 9–10). The second child was a daughter, and her name was to be Lo-ruhamah, which meant "not loved." The third child was a son whose name was Lo-ammi, which meant "not my people." Imagine these kids on the playground and being called "Hey, Not Loved," or "Hey, Not My People!" But those names served a purpose in the preaching by Hosea. He was also to tell the people that there was hope—that one day God's people would be called "My people," and "the ones I love."

But before that time, Gomer left Hosea and returned to her old life as a prostitute. Hosea is told to "go and love your wife again, even though she commits adultery with another lover" (Hos. 3:1). Again, Hosea's experience with Gomer was an illustration of what would happen with Israel. Someday, God and Israel would be in relationship again. Knowing that the relationship between God and Israel was the larger context of what Hosea was asked to do, there is also an interesting personal principle illustrated in what happened after Hosea redeemed Gomer for a pittance.

Apparently, her life of prostitution didn't support her, and she eventually sold herself into slavery. But the price Hosea pays to redeem her from slavery is small—she wasn't much of a slave at this point. She was sold back to Hosea at "half-price." But here's the interesting point for us. When Hosea brought her home, he told her, "You must live in my house for many days and stop your prostitution. During this time, you will not have sexual relations with anyone, not even me" (v. 3). The text continues on to the larger context, as it is compared to what Hosea was doing with what God would do with Israel. God said that Israel would "go a long time without a king or prince, and without sacrifices, sacred pillars, priests, or even idols!" (v. 4), referring to the coming exile of Israel by the Assyrians.

Let's look at the human part Hosea is called on to play. He brings Gomer home, but they do not immediately begin to act like husband and wife. There was to be a time of repair where trust could be rebuilt. Whenever I work with a couple where there has been unfaithfulness, I always refer the betrayed partner to Hosea 3:3. When the covenant bond has been broken, consequences follow. Trust has been destroyed. It only takes a moment for trust to vanish—but it takes a long time for trust to be rebuilt. And that is what Hosea was telling Gomer. There was no trust. There really wasn't a marital bond at this point. So Gomer must prove herself and begin the long process of rebuilding the trust she had destroyed by her return to her old life. No more prostitution—the old life is gone! But no sex between them either, for the bond of marriage has been broken and must be repaired over a period of time.

It's also interesting that God used prostitution, or sexual unfaithfulness, to describe his experience with Israel. He even says that Israel had gone "a whoring after [other] gods" (Exod. 34:16, *KJV*) The marriage relationship is the best analogy to Israel's relationship with God, just as it was with the apostle Paul's writings, who many times made that same correlation. We are the "bride of Christ" is his description of our relationship with God, just as Israel was in a covenantal relationship with Yahweh.

Hosea, the prophet, was called also to warn Israel about the coming doom, which occurred. In 722 BC, the Assyrians would destroy Israel and take the people captive.

Jonah

Everyone loves the story of Jonah. There are fun children's plays based on Jonah's story. Even those who know little about the Bible know the story of Jonah. So instead of reviewing the details of the book of Jonah, let's look at what the rabbis said about him. They claimed that in the very beginning God had created a great fish just for the purpose of eventually providing a home for Jonah for three days. They said the inside of this great fish was as big as a large synagogue, and that the eyes of the fish served as windows for Jonah. Inside the belly of the fish was a huge diamond, which provided light for the reluctant prophet. In their view, the inside of this great fish was luxurious, and Jonah apparently became quite comfortable inside the fish.

The rabbis also tell us that prior to God's calling Jonah to go to Nineveh, God had sent him to proclaim to the people of Jerusalem that unless they repented of their ways their great city was going to be destroyed. He must have been a quite a good preacher, for the people of Jerusalem listened to him, and repented. As a result, God changed his mind and had mercy on Jerusalem.

But the fact that destruction didn't fall upon Jerusalem meant that Jonah's prophecy didn't take place. This made Jonah a "false prophet," since what he had predicted just didn't happen. And that became Jonah's reputation. So when God called him to go to Nineveh and preach repentance, Jonah didn't trust that God would follow through. He felt that God had too soft a heart and was too willing to show mercy when the people repented. Jonah didn't want another "false prophet" label put on him, so he went the opposite direction—away from Nineveh. He got on a boat headed away from Nineveh and thought he was in the clear. But God sent a great storm that threatened everyone on the boat. The storm only stopped when the sailors threw Jonah overboard into the mouth of the great fish that was waiting for Jonah!

But after his sojourn in the belly of that great fish, Jonah made haste to get to Nineveh and preached his heart out. To the rabbis Nineveh was a "monster city" and contained 1.5 million people. Jonah's message was heard throughout the city, and repentance began when King Osnappar of Assyria, as the rabbis said, "descended from his throne, removed his crown, strewed ashes on his head instead, took off his purple garments and rolled about in the dust of the highways."[4] He set the example of repentance, and soon all the people in the city followed the king and repented.

Once again, what Jonah feared would happen, happened. Once again, Jonah was seen as a "false prophet," for what he had foretold didn't take place. Obviously, this made Jonah very angry with God. It's as if he said, "I knew it, God. You did it again! You showed mercy on the people of Nineveh." He complained to the Lord, and as he finished his complaint, he said he just wanted to die. He said, "Just kill me now, LORD! I'd rather be dead than alive if what I predicted will not happen" (Jonah 4:3). God's reply is interesting. One way of saying it is, "You do well to be angry—I understand." Jonah isn't rebuked for being angry, nor is he rebuked for expressing his anger.

After complaining to God, Jonah went and found a shady place where he could sit and pout. But overnight, God destroyed the plant that had given him shade, and once again Jonah was angry enough to want to die. This time God said, "I understand your anger because the plant died." Then God added, "You feel sorry about the plant, though you did nothing to put it there. It came quickly and died quickly. But Nineveh has more than 120,000 people living in spiritual darkness. . . . Shouldn't I feel sorry for such a great city?" (Jonah 4:10-11). God is saying to Jonah, "Trust me. Don't limit me by interpreting me through the circumstances, or even by the labels people put on you. Interpret the circumstance in light of your understanding of me!" In other words, God was telling Jonah that being a faithful "false" prophet was an honor, and that Jonah, since he was obedient, He, the merciful God, could show mercy.

Jeremiah

Jeremiah is unique among all the Old Testament prophets. He was the most open of all the prophets about what he experienced emotionally while acting in his role as a prophet. The other prophets delivered their message in a clear, precise and direct way. But they said little, if anything at all, about what they experienced as they fulfilled their role as a prophet. They did not record their personal involvement in their messages. Jeremiah, however, lays bare his emotions, and says over and over again how he weeps over what he is expected to tell the people. At one point, he says:

> When I speak, the words burst out. "Violence and de-struction!" I shout. So these messages from the LORD have made me a household joke. But if I say I'll never mention the LORD or speak in his name, his word burns in my heart like a fire. It's like a fire in my bones! I am worn out trying to hold it in! I can't do it! (Jer. 20:8-9).

He tried not to prophesy, but he couldn't keep silent. He knew that he was being mocked and ridiculed for his message, and he tried to shut up and lead a normal life. But he couldn't. God's message—God's Word—burned like a fire in his bones, and he could not keep silent. Wow! What a picture he paints with his words.

In the very first chapter of Jeremiah, we are told that even before he was born, God had selected him to be His spokesman. Jeremiah tried to beg off, based on his being too young for such a task. But God told him his age was irrelevant—he was to "go wherever I send you and say whatever I tell you. And don't be afraid of the people, for I will be with you and will protect you" (Jer. 1:7-8). Talk about a tough assignment! In short order, God showed Jeremiah that his message would be one of coming doom. His was a tough message, for unless the people repented, doom and disaster was the consequence.

As Jeremiah followed through and preached coming judgment, he prayed for the people and he wept over them. Finally, at one point, God told him to "pray no more for these people, Jeremiah. Do not weep or pray for them, for I will not listen to them when they cry out to me" (Jer. 11:14). What a hopeless task!

All of the prophets were called to what appeared to be a hopeless task. Jeremiah was to continue to preach the coming destruction of Jerusalem for almost 40 years. Five kings would sit on the throne of Judah during those years. Yet, I'm sure that as the time went on and on, and nothing happened, it looked like Jeremiah was the false prophet. The people were already complacent—becoming even more so as time passed.

One of the things the rabbis described as happening to Jeremiah was his encounter with Hananiah, who was also a prophet. At one point, Hananiah challenged Jeremiah in the Temple, saying that within two years, the God of Israel would "break the yoke that the king of Babylon [Nebuchadnezzar] has put on your necks" (Jer. 28:4). He gave a message directly opposite to what Jeremiah had been preaching.

Now at that time, Jeremiah was wearing a yoke around his neck to illustrate how the people would be wearing the yoke of Babylon. So he responded to Hananiah by saying, "I hope what you say comes true, but the role of the prophet has always been to speak words of warning." And then he added, "So a prophet who predicts peace must show he is right" (v. 9). In response to Jeremiah, Hananiah "took the yoke off Jeremiah's neck and broke it in pieces" (v. 10), and then repeated his prediction of peace. Jeremiah ended the conversation by saying that Hananiah would die before the end of the year. This conversation apparently took place during one of the Jewish fall festivals, and two months later, Hananiah died.

Now the rabbis described a later event when Jeremiah tried to leave the city while it was under siege, to make a visit to his hometown of Anathoth. The watchman at the gate stopped him and accused Jeremiah of being a traitor who intended to desert his own people and cross over to the enemy. His accusation ended with Jeremiah being put in prison, even though everyone knew the charge was untrue. But the rabbis point out that the watchman was the grandson of the false prophet Hananiah. As Hananiah was dying, he charged his son, Shelemiah, to seek every possible way to get revenge on Jeremiah, and it was his son, Irijah, who imprisoned Jeremiah. And he was even put in a prison where the jailer was a friend of the former Hananiah (see Jer. 37).

While Jeremiah was in prison, King Zedekiah, who had come to power at this time, needed to consult with him. In the meeting, Jeremiah asked to be released from prison and that the trumped-up charges against him be dropped. His wish was granted, but no sooner did he walk away a free man than the "nobility seized him and cast him into a lime pit filled with water, where they hoped he would drown. But a miracle happened. The water sank to the bottom, and the mud rose to the surface, and supported the prophet above the water"[5] (see Jer. 38). But after that, Jeremiah willingly spent the last days of Jerusalem in the palace prison courtyard, where King Zedekiah could protect him.

The rabbis said that for years, Nebuchadnezzar had been putting off the capture of Jerusalem. He was afraid of a repeat of the defeat of his predecessor Sennacherib, who had been sent running by the Lord during the reign of King Hezekiah (see 2 Kings 19:32-34). The rabbis added that God allowed the siege of Jerusalem to go on for almost three years, in hopes that the people would still repent. But they didn't, and so the inevitable happened—Jerusalem was destroyed. What Jeremiah had predicted with tears had finally come to pass. Jerusalem had fallen and Israel was in bondage.

We can really see Jeremiah's heart in his lament over the fall of that great city. Imagine what it must have been like when he returned to a burned and destroyed Jerusalem. What must it have been like to walk through the burned-out ruins and hear the cries of hunger from the children, and the desperate wail of the mothers who couldn't feed their children, let alone themselves? For almost 40 years, Jeremiah had warned the people, the nobility, the royalty, but no one listened. And now he sat in the ruins.

Read over the five chapters of the book of Lamentations and you can see the broken heart of an already emotional Jeremiah. Note especially the third chapter, where Jeremiah gives us a biblical picture of what a major depression feels like. He begins by saying:

> I am the one who has seen the afflictions that come from the rod of the LORD's anger. He has led me into darkness, shutting out all light. He has turned his hand against me again and again, all day long (Lam. 3:1-3).

In his depression, Jeremiah felt that all was darkness, and everyone was against him. And he felt like it was God who had turned everything and everyone against him. The prophet was broken by the terrible task he had been given by God. He continued:

> He has made my skin and flesh grow old. He has broken my bones. He has besieged and surrounded me with anguish and distress. He has buried me in a dark place, like those long dead (vv. 4-6).

Again, the darkness; only now it was even darker, for he felt like someone who had been buried alive. God was against him, and he was filled with anguish and distress. And as a result, his skin had become gray and old, and his bones ached and felt brittle.

He went on to describe how he was trapped—there was no place he could go to get away from his suffering. He was helpless and devastated—words often used by people to describe the desperation they feel as they are trapped in depression.

Then he talked about how the people had made fun of him, even mocking him and his message in songs. He was even grinding his teeth, and it felt like he was chewing on gravel. Finally, he said:

> Peace has been stripped away, and I have forgotten what prosperity is. I cry out, "My splendor is gone! Everything I had hoped for from the LORD is lost." The thought of my suffering and homelessness is bitter beyond words (vv. 17-19).

All hope is gone, and Jeremiah is left with hopelessness. But there is a break at verse 21. Suddenly, in the midst of this horrible depression, he changed his focus. He said:

> Yet I still dare to hope when I remember this: The faithful love of the LORD never ends! His mercies never cease. Great is his faithfulness; his mercies begin afresh each morning.

I say to myself, "The LORD is my inheritance; therefore,
I will hope in him!" (vv. 21-24).

Picture him, sitting perhaps on a burnt and blackened concrete block, weeping as he looked around. And then, perhaps it
was the word "hope" that made him stop looking around, and
look up. As Jeremiah recaptured God's perspective, he saw that
God had done exactly what He had said He would do through the
messages given by him to proclaim. Suddenly he realized that God
was still God. It was the realization of what we've talked about before. He shifted his perception from what was in front of him to
the One who had been walking beside him all those years. He
shifted his gaze from the devastation to the faithfulness of God
to those who would keep His covenant. And today we have that
great hymn of God's faithfulness based on Jeremiah's renewed
vision of God.

So What Can We Learn?

Let's begin with Elijah. We left him depressed, waiting for God to
speak to him. When that happened, Elijah learned there were four
things God had for him to do. They are what we need to do when
we feel down, discouraged or depressed.

First, he needed to *get something to eat and drink*. Depression usually affects our appetite—we don't care whether or not we eat—but
the angel of the Lord said, "Get up and eat" (1 Kings 19:5). And
suddenly there was a fresh loaf of bread next to him—another miracle. Then the angel said again, "Get up and eat some more, or the
journey ahead will be too much for you" (v. 7). So that's the second
thing God confronted Elijah with—*get up—set a goal—do something*!
The angel of the Lord told him he had something he had to do—
so get busy. Elijah's goal was to get to Mount Sinai, which was
about 200 miles away.

The third thing Elijah needed to do was to *slow down and listen
for the voice of God*. Even though he was depressed he needed to get
back to his relationship with God. God was going to show him

His side of what had happened in Israel. He was going to correct Elijah's thinking. Elijah thought he was the only one loyal to Yahweh, but he was going to find out that there were 7,000 others in Israel who had never bowed a knee to Baal. Perhaps Elijah also remembered what Obadiah had told him—how he had protected and preserved the lives of 100 faithful prophets.

Depression can be a "thought" disorder—it certainly becomes that. When we are depressed we can't see much else than what has knocked us down. We think only about the problem, not the Provider. As we said in an earlier chapter, we need to begin with God, and then interpret our circumstances in light of who and what God is, not define God by our circumstances. Elijah needed to get his eyes focused on the right thing—on God's point of view, not Jezebel's.

Finally, the fourth thing Elijah was to do was to *team up with someone.* No longer was he to go it alone. So on the way home he was told to team up with Elisha and do his prophetic work in partnership. Elisha became Elijah's assistant. Depression leads us into the state of aloneness and isolation. We cut off the people we need to be part of our life. We even ignore our "accountability partners." For as the proverb says, "Each heart knows its own bitterness, and no one else can fully share its joy" (Prov. 14:10). I've always been struck by the pairing of "bitterness" and "joy" in that proverb. It highlights our tendency to go it alone when we are bitter and depressed. But God says, "Get someone else in your life and let them share your journey!"

When we look at the other three prophets we've discussed, we see several other things. Both Jeremiah and Jonah had to deal with depression. For them, the answer was to stay faithful. Hosea was to stay faithful in his relationship with Gomer, even though it must have been very painful. For each of these prophets life was tough. None of these prophets was called to a "blessed" life where there were few or no problems. In fact, their lives became more complicated because of their obedience. But in the midst of their tough situations they learned that God was faithful. What He promised, He delivered, even when it looked like He did the opposite. We need to be careful and not miss that message when our life gets tough. God is faithful, and we need to hold onto that truth no matter what—even when our situation seems overwhelming.

The other thing we can learn from these prophets is that God is patient with our struggles. Not once do we read that God judged or became impatient or was even bothered by their frustrations. Read through the book of Jeremiah and you will see that each time Jeremiah complained, God listened and responded. Sometimes we are afraid to be honest with the God, who already knows our innermost thoughts. How incongruent is that idea! If God knows our hearts we can be completely honest with Him about everything we are experiencing. We just need to keep in mind the principle that we are not to change our understanding of God based on our circumstances. We let God continue to be God.

We've looked at the stories of 18 of the people of the Bible. In each of their stories we can find something that can apply to our lives. But we also can see that as we look at their lives we are able to enrich our knowledge and understanding of the God of the Bible. Their stories are really stories about the God of the Bible. May His story not only enrich your life, but expand and enrich your relationship with the God of the Old Testament—the living Yahweh. The great "I AM that I AM!"

Small-Group and Individual

STUDY GUIDE

To enrich your understanding of these biblical characters, the following questions are for you to work on individually, or even better, to discuss together in a small group. If you are doing this in a small group, spend some time thinking through the questions on your own, and then discuss your responses together.

CHAPTER 1
ABRAHAM: THE IMPERFECT FATHER OF OUR FAITH

1. What do you remember about the time when you first came to faith in God?

_____

_____

_____

_____

_____

2. Has there been an area in your faith-walk where you have consistently struggled?

_____

_____

_____

_____

_____

3. When has your faith been the strongest? Why do you think that is true?

_____

_____

_____

_____

_____

4. When has your faith been the weakest? Why do you think that is true?

_____

_____

_____

_____

_____

5. What are some things you are doing in order to strengthen your faith?

_____

_____

_____

_____

_____

_____

CHAPTER 2
ISAAC: THE SILENT SAINT

1. What do you remember about your father when you were about 10 years old?

_____

_____

_____

_____

_____

_____

2. What do you wish your father had done differently when you were that age?

_____

_____

_____

_____

_____

_____

3. If your father is still alive, what is your relationship with him like today?

_____

_____

_____

_____
_____
_____

4. In what ways did your father contribute, either positively or negatively, to your faith-walk?

_____
_____
_____
_____
_____
_____

5. Did you have other father figures growing up? If so, how were they different from your father?

_____
_____
_____
_____
_____
_____

CHAPTER 3
JACOB: THE FEARFUL SAINT

1. How have you struggled with fear in your life?

_____
_____
_____
_____
_____
_____

2. Are there fears you have overcome? How were you able to defeat those fears?

_____

_____

_____

_____

_____

_____

3. Have you ever felt that God surprised you by His presence in a situation? How?

_____

_____

_____

_____

_____

_____

4. What promises of God have you held onto in the presence of fear?

_____

_____

_____

_____

_____

_____

5. Describe a time, when you look back on it, that you can see God's hand at work, even though at the time you were not aware of His presence.

_____

_____

_____

_____

_____

Chapter 4
The Family Dynamics of Jacob and Esau

1. If Abraham's family was dysfunctional, how does that help you have courage to look at your own family dynamics?

_____

_____

_____

_____

_____

_____

2. Typically, do you struggle more with fear or with anger?

_____

_____

_____

_____

3. Who were you closer to when growing up—your mom or your dad? How do you think that affects your struggle with either fear or anger as an adult?

_____

_____

_____

_____

_____

4. Were your family dynamics stronger in the attachment task or the autonomy task?

_____

_____

_____

_____

5. How much "Esau" or "Jacob" do you have in you in regard to your family relationships?

_____

_____

_____

_____

_____

CHAPTER 5
JOSEPH: THE VICTIMIZED SAINT

1. Who was the favored child in your family as you were growing up? How did it affect you?

_____

_____

_____

_____

_____

2. What are some of the things your family never talked about, and maybe still will not talk about?

_____

_____

_____

_____

_____

3. We know the end of Joseph's story, but we don't know the end of our own stories. What are some of the "dots" you still can't connect in your story?

_____

_____

_____

_____

_____

4. When have you felt "forgotten by God"? Has anything about that period of time now started to make sense to you spiritually?

_____

_____

_____

_____

_____

5. If you could honestly affirm that "the Lord has always been with me," how would that affect your faith-walk?

_____

_____

_____

_____

_____

_____

CHAPTER 6
JOB: THE ARGUMENTATIVE SAINT

1. How do you explain to yourself God's purpose in allowing suffering?

_____

_____

_____

_____

2. What are some of the "doubts" you have in your faith?

_____

_____

_____

_____

_____

3. How comfortable are you with arguing with God? How has seeing Job's struggle helped you become more comfortable with arguing with God?

_____

_____

_____

_____

_____

4. Have you ever been "comforted" by someone who used the "religion argument" in his or her attempt to comfort you? How did that affect you?

_____

_____

_____

_____

_____

5. How "big" is your understanding of God?

_____

_____

_____

_____

_____

CHAPTER 7
MOSES: THE RELUCTANT SAINT

1. What do you think it means when C. S. Lewis says, "God is good, but he is not safe"?

_____

_____

_____

_____

_____

_____

2. Have you ever been reluctant to follow the Lord? What held you back?

_____

_____

_____

_____

_____

3. How have you struggled, or do you struggle, with self-doubt, like Moses?

_____

_____

_____

_____

_____

4. How would you describe the "glory of God" as referenced, for example, in Psalm 19, or in the Israelites' experience in the desert?

_____

_____

_____

_____

_____

5. What hinders your faith-walk in a way that in turn hinders your intimacy with God?

_____

_____

_____

_____

_____

CHAPTER 8
SAMSON: THE PAMPERED SAINT

1. How would you describe the parenting skills of Manoah and his wife?

   _____

   _____

   _____

   _____

   _____

   _____

2. How is Samson an example of the sexual impurity of our age?

   _____

   _____

   _____

   _____

   _____

3. Since God still used Samson, why is sexual purity important?

   _____

   _____

   _____

   _____

   _____

4. Why was it so hard for Samson to "get it"? Why is it so hard for us at times to "get it"?

   _____

   _____

   _____

   _____

   _____

5. Is there an area in your life where you are resisting God because you feel inadequate?

_____
_____
_____
_____
_____
_____

CHAPTER 9
SAMUEL: THE JEALOUS SAINT

1. How have you struggled with "hearing God speak"?

_____
_____
_____
_____
_____

2. Hannah so wanted a son that she was willing to give him up. Have you ever wanted something so bad that you were willing to give it up? What happened?

_____
_____
_____
_____
_____

3. Describe a time when it was difficult for you to wait.

_____
_____
_____
_____
_____

4. Does it surprise you that the great prophet Samuel had weaknesses? How do you think he overcame his weaknesses?

_____

_____

_____

_____

_____

5. How can you be a better listener to God's voice?

_____

_____

_____

_____

_____

CHAPTER 10
KING SAUL: THE "COULD HAVE BEEN" SAINT

1. Have you ever been tempted to change a belief in order to accept a wrong behavior?

_____

_____

_____

_____

2. What personal examples can you give for each of the three categories of belief: public, private and core beliefs?

_____

_____

_____

_____

_____

3. Have you ever hidden from a challenge? How? Why?

_____

_____

_____

_____

_____

_____

4. How does the principle "to obey is better than sacrifice" operate in your life? What are some of the hard choices you've faced?

_____

_____

_____

_____

_____

_____

5. Describe how you are not like Saul.

_____

_____

_____

_____

_____

_____

CHAPTER 11
DAVID: THE SINFUL SAINT

1. How do you understand the words God said about David—"a man after my own heart"?

_____

_____

_____

_____

_____

2. How does an understanding of David's dark side help you accept your dark side?

_____

_____

_____

_____

_____

_____

_____

3. What happens to you when your challenges are met? Are you bored, or calm?

_____

_____

_____

_____

_____

_____

_____

4. Is there a Nathan in your life? Who is it?

_____

_____

_____

_____

_____

5. What does it mean for one to have a "soft heart"?

_____

_____

_____

_____

_____

_____

CHAPTER 12
SOME SAINTLY WOMEN

1. Can you think of a time when you defined God by your circumstances? Describe it.

_____

_____

_____

_____

_____

_____

2. Describe a situation when you defined your circumstances in light of who God is.

_____

_____

_____

_____

_____

3. How has our culture today impacted your church? Your faith?

_____

_____

_____

_____

_____

4. Who is walking at your side in your walk of faith?

_____

_____

_____

_____

_____

5. Where and when do you still struggle to have a "willing heart?"

_____

_____

_____

_____

_____

CHAPTER 13
SOME SAINTS WHO WERE PROPHETS

1. How comfortable are you with your emotions? What emotion are you most uncomfortable with?

_____

_____

_____

_____

_____

2. How would you respond to a call from God to fail, as Jeremiah's call was? What would you do?

_____

_____

_____

_____

_____

3. Why do you think Elijah was so afraid of Jezebel? Do you have someone in your life like her?

_____

_____

_____

_____

_____

4. How do you explain that in Jonah's eyes success in God's plan for him was a failure?

_____

_____

_____

_____

_____

_____

5. How do you change your self-talk as Jeremiah did in Lamentations 3? How could you switch from brooding over the horrible circumstances to dwelling on God's faithfulness and mercy in a situation in your own life?

_____

_____

_____

_____

_____

_____

ENDNOTES

Introduction

1. Eugene Peterson, *Practice Resurrection* (Grand Rapids, MI: Wm. B. Eerdmans Publishing Co., 2010), p. 78.

Chapter 1—Abraham: The Imperfect Father of Our Faith

1. Louis Ginzberg, *The Legends of the Jews, Vol. 1* (The Jewish Publication Society of America, 2010).
2. Lippman Bodoff, *Who's Testing Whom*, quoted in Herschel Shanks, *Abraham and Family* (Washington DC: Biblical Archeology Society, 2000), pp. 13-20.
3. Ibid., p. 15.
4. Ibid., p. 18.
5. Walter Brueggemann, *Genesis: Interpretation: A Bible Commentary for Teaching and Preaching* (Atlanta, GA: John Knox Press, 1982), p. 113.
6. Eugene Peterson, *The Way of Jesus* (Grand Rapids, MI: Eerdmans, 2007), p. 57.

Chapter 2—Isaac: The Silent Saint

1. Written in 1843 and available in various translations.
2. Frederick Buechner, *Son of Laughter* (New York: HarperCollins, 1994).
3. Augusten Burroughs, *A Wolf at the Table*, (New York: St. Martin's Press, 2008), p. 186.

Chapter 3—Jacob: The Fearful Saint

1. Lawrence Kushner, *God Was in This Place & I, I Did Not Know: Finding Self, Spirituality, and Ultimate Meaning* (Woodstock, VT: Jewish Lights Publishing, 1991), p. 110.
2. Walter Brueggemann, *Genesis: Interpretation: A Bible Commentary for Teaching and Preaching* (Atlanta, GA: John Knox Press, 1982), p. 270.
3. Ibid., p. 210.

Chapter 4—The Family Dynamics of Jacob and Esau

1. See more of my story in my book *Making Peace with Your Father,* Regal Books, Ventura, CA, 2004.

Chapter 5—Joseph: The Victimized Saint

1. For more on this, see David Stoop, *Forgiving the Unforgivable* (Regal Books, Ventura, CA, 1991, 2011).
2. B. Yoma 35b; *Test of Joseph ix, 5;* Gen. Rab. 1075,76: a tractate of the Mishna and the Babylonian Talmud. Quoted in Graves, Robert and Patai, Raphael, *Hebrew Myths*, Greenwich House, New York, 1963, pp. 254,255.

3. Walter Breuggemann, *Genesis: Interpretation: A Bible Commentary for Teaching and Preaching,* (Atlanta, GA: John Knox Press, 1982), p. 289.

Chapter 6—Job: The Argumentative Saint
1. Louis Ginzberg, *The Legends of the Jews, Vol. 2* (The Jewish Publication Society of America, 2010), p. 227.
2. Edmond Fleg, *The Life of Moses* (Pasadena, CA: Hope Publishing House, 1995).
3. Anson Laytner, *Arguing with God: a Jewish Tradition,* (NJ: Jason Aronson, 1990), p. 3.

Chapter 7—Moses: The Reluctant Saint
1. C. S. Lewis, *The Lion, the Witch, and the Wardrobe* (England: Penguin Books, 1950), p. 71.
2. Edmond Fleg, *The Life of Moses* (Pasadena, CA: Hope Publishing House, 1995).
3. Jonathan Kirsch, *Moses, A Life* (New York: Ballantine Books, 1998), p. 130.
4. Levi Meier, *Moses, the Prince, the Prophet* (Woodstock, VT: Jewish Lights Publishing, 1999), p. 42.
5. Kirsch, *Moses, A Life,* p. 2
6. Ibid., p. 13

Chapter 8—Samson: The Pampered Saint
1. Janice Shaw Crouse, PhD, "Pornography and Sex Trafficking," Concerned Women for America. http://www.cwfa.org/articledisplay.asp?id=15208&department=BLI&categoryid=dotcommentary&subcategoryid=blitraf.
2. "Pornography Statistics 2003" Internet Filter Review, 2004. http://www.internetfilter-review.com/internet-pornography-statistics.html.
3. Walt Mueller, "Teens and Pornography: Always Bad, Getting Worse," Center for Parent/Youth Understanding, 2005. http://www.cpyu.org/Page.aspx?id=163417.
4. Kelsey Castanon, "Addicted: Diagnostic Manual Classifies Sexual Compulsion as Disorder," May 5, 2001, http://www.kstatecollegian.com/news/addicted-1.2559700; "Pastors Discuss Their Sexual Addiction in TV Documentary," ChristianNewsWire, http://www.christiannewswire.com/news/550498060.html.
5. Louis Ginzberg, *The Legends of the Jews, Vol. 4* (The Jewish Publication Society of America, 2010), p. 48.

Chapter 9—Samuel: The Jealous Saint
1. Bill Hybels, *The Power of a Whisper* (Grand Rapids, MI: Zondervan, 2010), p. 22.

Chapter 10—King Saul: The "Could Have Been" Saint
1. Louis Ginzberg, *The Legends of the Jews, Vol. 4* (The Jewish Publication Society of America, 2010), p. 68.

Chapter 11—David: The Sinful Saint
1. Louis Ginzberg, *The Legends of the Jews, Vol. 4* (The Jewish Publication Society of America, 2010), p. 82.
2. Ibid., p. 103.
3. Walter Brueggemann, *Genesis: Interpretation: A Bible Commentary for Teaching and Preaching* (Atlanta, GA: John Knox Press, 1982), p. 272.
4. Ibid.

Chapter 12—Some Saintly Women
1. Paul Tournier, *To Resist or to Surrender?* (Richmond, VA: John Knox Press, 1964), p. 8.
2. Frederick Buechner, *Peculiar Treasures* (NY: HarperCollins, 1979), p. 27.

3. Louis Ginzberg, *The Legends of the Jews, Vol. 4* (The Jewish Publication Society of America, 2010), p. 35.

4. Ibid., p. 391.

5. Ibid., p. 388.

Chapter 13—Some Saints Who Were Prophets

1. Louis Ginzberg, *The Legends of the Jews, Vol. 4* (The Jewish Publication Society of America, 2010), p. 196.

2. Ibid., p. 201.

3. Ibid., p. 223.

4. Ibid., p. 250.

5. Ibid., p. 299.

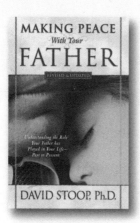

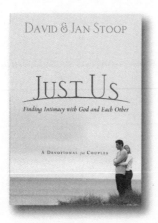